Whispers of Wisdom: A Divine Feminine Reflection on The Book of Proverbs

Joseline Jean-Louis Hardrick

Published by Joseline Hardrick, 2025.

WHISPERS OF WISDOM: A DIVINE FEMININE REFLECTION ON THE BOOK OF PROVERBS

First edition. August 26, 2025.

Copyright © 2025 Joseline Jean-Louis Hardrick.

ISBN: 978-1958912584

Written by Joseline Jean-Louis Hardrick.

To all those seeking wisdom.

Preface

Dear Reader,

These whispers are sacred.

Born from joy, built on grace, and passed through hands that healed through fire.

Use them daily. Record them in your voice. Share them with your babies.

Sleep to them.

Wake to them.

Let them remind you who you are—every sunrise, every sundown.

You don't have to be loud to be powerful.

You just have to be present.

With softness & sovereignty,

—Your Favorite Auntie of Affirmation

Introduction

There is a quiet kind of power that comes not from shouting, but from whispering truth to yourself until you finally believe it.

This book was born in the hush between chaos and clarity, in the stillness where Spirit speaks. Whispers of Wisdom is more than a devotional—it's a daily practice of reclaiming your peace, honoring your power, and anchoring your soul. It's that deep breath before the world starts pulling on you. It's the exhale you didn't know you'd been holding all day. It's your auntie's wisdom, your therapist's gentleness, and your ancestors' strength—wrapped in poetry and permission.

Each day, you'll be invited to start your morning with intention and end your evening with affirmation. The structure is simple, but the shift is sacred:

- Sunrise whispers to ground your spirit before the noise.
- Sunset whispers to soothe your soul before the stillness.

These whispers are rooted in ancient truth—some inspired by the Book of Proverbs, others grown from the soil of lived experience. They speak in the language of the now but echo wisdom from generations of women who've survived, thrived, and dared to rest.

Note

The version of the Book of Proverbs used in this text is the World English Bible, this modern English translation is based on the ASV and is explicitly in the public domain. It aims for a balance of accuracy and readability. The reimaginings are my own.

Proverbs 1

1 The proverbs of Solomon, the son of David, king of Israel:
2 to know wisdom and instruction;
to discern the words of understanding;
3 to receive instruction in wise dealing,
in righteousness, justice, and equity;
4 to give prudence to the simple,
knowledge and discretion to the young man—
5 that the wise man may hear, and increase in learning;
that the man of understanding may attain to sound counsel;
6 to understand a proverb and parables,
the words and riddles of the wise.
7 The fear of Yahweh† is the beginning of knowledge,
but the foolish despise wisdom and instruction.
8 My son, listen to your father's instruction,
and don't forsake your mother's teaching;
9 for they will be a garland to grace your head,
and chains around your neck.
10 My son, if sinners entice you,
don't consent.
11 If they say, "Come with us.
Let's lie in wait for blood.
Let's lurk secretly for the innocent without cause.
12 Let's swallow them up alive like Sheol,‡
and whole, like those who go down into the pit.
13 We'll find all valuable wealth.
We'll fill our houses with plunder.

14 You shall cast your lot among us.
We'll all have one purse"—
15 my son, don't walk on the path with them.
Keep your foot from their path,
16 for their feet run to evil.
They hurry to shed blood.
17 For the net is spread in vain in the sight of any bird;
18 but these lay in wait for their own blood.
They lurk secretly for their own lives.
19 So are the ways of everyone who is greedy for gain.
It takes away the life of its owners.
20 Wisdom calls aloud in the street.
She utters her voice in the public squares.
21 She calls at the head of noisy places.
At the entrance of the city gates, she utters her words:
22 "How long, you simple ones, will you love simplicity?
How long will mockers delight themselves in mockery,
and fools hate knowledge?
23 Turn at my reproof.
Behold,§ I will pour out my spirit on you.
I will make known my words to you.
24 Because I have called, and you have refused;
I have stretched out my hand, and no one has paid attention;
25 but you have ignored all my counsel,
and wanted none of my reproof;
26 I also will laugh at your disaster.
I will mock when calamity overtakes you,
27 when calamity overtakes you like a storm,
when your disaster comes on like a whirlwind,
when distress and anguish come on you.
28 Then they will call on me, but I will not answer.
They will seek me diligently, but they will not find me,
29 because they hated knowledge,
and didn't choose the fear of Yahweh.
30 They wanted none of my counsel.

They despised all my reproof.
31 Therefore they will eat of the fruit of their own way,
and be filled with their own schemes.
32 For the backsliding of the simple will kill them.
The careless ease of fools will destroy them.
33 But whoever listens to me will dwell securely,
and will be at ease, without fear of harm."

Day 1 – Whispers

Proverbs 1 — The Whisper of Wisdom

"The fear of Yahweh is the beginning of knowledge; but the foolish despise wisdom and instruction."

— Proverbs 1:7 (WEB)

REFLECTION:

It begins not with knowing—but with honoring.
　　With bowing your head before you puff your chest.
　　Wisdom don't shout in the streets just to hear herself talk—
　　She's calling, whispering, waiting on the corners
　　For the ones bold enough to listen.
　　But fools?
　　Fools treat wisdom like spam mail.
　　Like an old woman rambling on the porch
　　When really, she's been holding the key all along.
　　Don't be so educated that you forget how to reverence.
　　Don't be so grown that you stop being teachable.
　　Truth knocks softly—respect is what turns the knob.
　　Selah.

Sunrise: The Dawn Knows Your Name

Rise slow. Breathe deep. You are not behind. The sun doesn't rush, yet it always shines on time.

She sets intention before she speaks. Her words bloom peace, not weeds.

He walks steady, even when the path sways. Truth is his compass, grace his pace.

They do not chase what's not meant for them. What's for them will recognize their name.

Your quiet is powerful. Let silence finish what noise could never start.

As you step into this day, carry these whispers with you. Repeat the ones that speak to your spirit. Forget the ones that don't. Either way, the wisdom stays with you. You're not alone in this.

Sunset: The Night Still Sees You

You did enough. You are enough. Lay it down. Tomorrow will rise with new mercy.

She forgives herself in whispers, not shouts. That's how healing finds its way in.

He does not carry every burden home. Some things belong to the wind.

They rest like roots—unseen, but growing. Stillness is strategy, not surrender.

Close your eyes, not your heart. Love still works the night shift.

Let these whispers wrap around you. Let them cradle the parts of you the world forgets to hold. You are sacred. You are safe. You are still becoming.

Proverb 2

1 My son, if you will receive my words,
and store up my commandments within you,
2 so as to turn your ear to wisdom,
and apply your heart to understanding;
3 yes, if you call out for discernment,
and lift up your voice for understanding;
4 if you seek her as silver,
and search for her as for hidden treasures;
5 then you will understand the fear of Yahweh,
and find the knowledge of God.†
6 For Yahweh gives wisdom.
Out of his mouth comes knowledge and understanding.
7 He lays up sound wisdom for the upright.
He is a shield to those who walk in integrity,
8 that he may guard the paths of justice,
and preserve the way of his saints.
9 Then you will understand righteousness and justice,
equity and every good path.
10 For wisdom will enter into your heart.
Knowledge will be pleasant to your soul.
11 Discretion will watch over you.
Understanding will keep you,
12 to deliver you from the way of evil,
from the men who speak perverse things,
13 who forsake the paths of uprightness,
to walk in the ways of darkness,

14 who rejoice to do evil,
and delight in the perverseness of evil,
15 who are crooked in their ways,
and wayward in their paths,
16 to deliver you from the strange woman,
even from the foreigner who flatters with her words,
17 who forsakes the friend of her youth,
and forgets the covenant of her God;
18 for her house leads down to death,
her paths to the departed spirits.
19 None who go to her return again,
neither do they attain to the paths of life.
20 Therefore walk in the way of good men,
and keep the paths of the righteous.
21 For the upright will dwell in the land.
The perfect will remain in it.
22 But the wicked will be cut off from the land.
The treacherous will be rooted out of it.

Day 2 – Whispers

Proverbs 2 — Hidden in the Soil

"Yes, if you cry after discernment, and lift up your voice for understanding; if you seek her as silver, and search for her as for hidden treasures: then you will understand the fear of Yahweh, and find the knowledge of God."

— Proverbs 2:3–5 (WEB)

Reflection:

Wisdom don't chill on the surface like sidewalk pennies.
You gotta dig for her.
Get your knees dirty.
Turn over the soil of your soul until something sacred stirs.
She ain't hiding to punish you—
She's hiding because the journey makes you ready.
Not everything holy is obvious.
Not everything deep comes loud.
So go get your shovel, child.
Cry out, reach up, dig down.
Silver can tarnish, but wisdom glows in the dark.
Selah.

Sunrise: Worth Wakes With You

You are not valuable because you are busy. You are valuable because you are here.

The world may overlook you. But wisdom never will.

She does not rush to be seen. She stands still, and the light finds her.

He is not a machine. He is a miracle. Rest is his birthright.

They don't need to hustle to prove they matter. They breathe. That's enough.

Let this day meet the whole you—not the edited version. You don't have to earn your existence. You woke up. That's a blessing. Now walk in it.

Sunset: You Are More Than What You Do

Your worth is not measured in tasks checked off. It is etched into your spirit.

She did what she could. That's enough.

He left some things undone. Still worthy. Still whole.

They are not a project. They are a person. Let that be enough tonight.

The world may forget, but your soul remembers: You are more than what you do.

Let this night hold you like a soft hand on your back. Close your eyes. You are not your performance. You are precious. Just as you are.

Proverbs 3

1 My son, don't forget my teaching,
   but let your heart keep my commandments,
   2 for they will add to you length of days,
   years of life, and peace.
   3 Don't let kindness and truth forsake you.
   Bind them around your neck.
   Write them on the tablet of your heart.
   4 So you will find favor,
   and good understanding in the sight of God and man.
   5 Trust in Yahweh with all your heart,
   and don't lean on your own understanding.
   6 In all your ways acknowledge him,
   and he will make your paths straight.
   7 Don't be wise in your own eyes.
   Fear Yahweh, and depart from evil.
   8 It will be health to your body,
   and nourishment to your bones.
   9 Honor Yahweh with your substance,
   with the first fruits of all your increase;
   10 so your barns will be filled with plenty,
   and your vats will overflow with new wine.
   11 My son, don't despise Yahweh's discipline,
   neither be weary of his correction;
   12 for whom Yahweh loves, he corrects,
   even as a father reproves the son in whom he delights.
   13 Happy is the man who finds wisdom,

the man who gets understanding.
14 For her good profit is better than getting silver,
and her return is better than fine gold.
15 She is more precious than rubies.
None of the things you can desire are to be compared to her.
16 Length of days is in her right hand.
In her left hand are riches and honor.
17 Her ways are ways of pleasantness.
All her paths are peace.
18 She is a tree of life to those who lay hold of her.
Happy is everyone who retains her.
19 By wisdom Yahweh founded the earth.
By understanding, he established the heavens.
20 By his knowledge, the depths were broken up,
and the skies drop down the dew.
21 My son, let them not depart from your eyes.
Keep sound wisdom and discretion,
22 so they will be life to your soul,
and grace for your neck.
23 Then you shall walk in your way securely.
Your foot won't stumble.
24 When you lie down, you will not be afraid.
Yes, you will lie down, and your sleep will be sweet.
25 Don't be afraid of sudden fear,
neither of the desolation of the wicked, when it comes;
26 for Yahweh will be your confidence,
and will keep your foot from being taken.
27 Don't withhold good from those to whom it is due,
when it is in the power of your hand to do it.
28 Don't say to your neighbor, "Go, and come again;
tomorrow I will give it to you,"
when you have it by you.
29 Don't devise evil against your neighbor,
since he dwells securely by you.
30 Don't strive with a man without cause,

if he has done you no harm.

31 Don't envy the man of violence.
Choose none of his ways.

32 For the perverse is an abomination to Yahweh,
but his friendship is with the upright.

33 Yahweh's curse is in the house of the wicked,
but he blesses the habitation of the righteous.

34 Surely he mocks the mockers,
but he gives grace to the humble.

35 The wise will inherit glory,
but shame will be the promotion of fools.

Day 3 – Whispers

Proverbs 3 — Trust Ain't Transactional

"Trust in Yahweh with all your heart, and don't lean on your own understanding. In all your ways acknowledge him, and he will make your paths straight."

— Proverbs 3:5–6 (WEB)

Reflection:

Trust ain't a trade. It's a surrender.

It's unclenching your fists and saying,

"Okay, I don't get it—but I'm still gon' go."

Your understanding got you here.

But it won't get you there.

Sometimes the path don't straighten 'til your knees hit the ground.

Sometimes the detour *is* the direction.

And the straight path?

It's not always short. It's just sure.

So lean in—not on logic, but on love.

And walk even when the fog won't clear.

Selah.

Sunrise: Your Light Don't Lie

You don't have to shrink to fit. You are the shape of something sacred.

Her glow is not arrogance. It's ancestry. It's earned.

He shines quietly. Let that be enough.

They radiate when they rest in truth. And truth don't need applause.

Your light don't lie. Let it lead today.

Walk like the sun chose you. Speak like your words make worlds. Your light ain't loud—but it sure is lasting.

Sunset: It's Safe to Dim Tonight

Not every light shines all night. Some flicker. Some sleep. All are worthy.

She doesn't perform peace. She practices it.

He turned off the noise. And found himself in the hush.

They dimmed their glow. Not to hide, but to heal.

Rest is not retreat. It's remembering who you are.

You don't have to defend yourself in your dreams. Sleep soft. Let Spirit guard what you've been carrying.

Proverbs 4

1 Listen, sons, to a father's instruction.
Pay attention and know understanding;
2 for I give you sound learning.
Don't forsake my law.
3 For I was a son to my father,
tender and an only child in the sight of my mother.
4 He taught me, and said to me:
"Let your heart retain my words.
Keep my commandments, and live.
5 Get wisdom.
Get understanding.
Don't forget, and don't deviate from the words of my mouth.
6 Don't forsake her, and she will preserve you.
Love her, and she will keep you.
7 Wisdom is supreme.
Get wisdom.
Yes, though it costs all your possessions, get understanding.
8 Esteem her, and she will exalt you.
She will bring you to honor when you embrace her.
9 She will give to your head a garland of grace.
She will deliver a crown of splendor to you."
10 Listen, my son, and receive my sayings.
The years of your life will be many.
11 I have taught you in the way of wisdom.
I have led you in straight paths.
12 When you go, your steps will not be hampered.

When you run, you will not stumble.
13 Take firm hold of instruction.
Don't let her go.
Keep her, for she is your life.
14 Don't enter into the path of the wicked.
Don't walk in the way of evil men.
15 Avoid it, and don't pass by it.
Turn from it, and pass on.
16 For they don't sleep unless they do evil.
Their sleep is taken away, unless they make someone fall.
17 For they eat the bread of wickedness
and drink the wine of violence.
18 But the path of the righteous is like the dawning light
that shines more and more until the perfect day.
19 The way of the wicked is like darkness.
They don't know what they stumble over.
20 My son, attend to my words.
Turn your ear to my sayings.
21 Let them not depart from your eyes.
Keep them in the center of your heart.
22 For they are life to those who find them,
and health to their whole body.
23 Keep your heart with all diligence,
for out of it is the wellspring of life.
24 Put away from yourself a perverse mouth.
Put corrupt lips far from you.
25 Let your eyes look straight ahead.
Fix your gaze directly before you.
26 Make the path of your feet level.
Let all of your ways be established.
27 Don't turn to the right hand nor to the left.
Remove your foot from evil.

Day 4 – Whispers

Proverbs 4 — Guard the Garden

"Keep your heart with all diligence, for out of it is the wellspring of life."
— Proverbs 4:23 (WEB)

Reflection:
Your heart is a garden, beloved.
And everybody don't deserve a key.
Some want to pluck your fruit without planting a seed.
Others try to leave their weeds behind.
So guard it—not with walls, but with wisdom.
Not out of fear, but out of reverence.
Because everything flows from here:
Your joy. Your peace. Your vision. Your voice.
If you don't tend to your heart,
the whole field turns wild.
So water it with truth.
Pull up bitterness by the root.
And never forget—you are the keeper of your own soil.
Selah.

Sunrise: Listen First, Speak Soft

Listen first, even if your thoughts shout. Wisdom is patient. She don't interrupt.

Her silence says more than noise ever could.

He speaks softly, but carries clarity. No need to roar to be heard.

They don't match volume with volume. They match energy with intention.

A soft word can crack the hardest heart. Speak it, then step back.

You don't have to fight for every word to land. Let wisdom whisper through you today. Be still enough to hear her.

Sunset: Release the Need to Explain

She explained herself to exhaustion. Now she lets her peace speak first.

He stopped editing his truth for comfort. Freedom followed.

They realized not everyone will understand. And that's okay.

Your spirit don't need defending. Let it be.

You don't need to be understood to be whole. Release. Rest.

You've earned the right to rest without a dissertation. No more proving, baby. Let peace be the only thing you carry to bed.

Proverbs 5

¹ My son, pay attention to my wisdom.
  Turn your ear to my understanding,

  ² that you may maintain discretion,
  that your lips may preserve knowledge.

  ³ For the lips of an adulteress drip honey.
  Her mouth is smoother than oil,

  ⁴ but in the end she is as bitter as wormwood,
  and as sharp as a two-edged sword.

  ⁵ Her feet go down to death.

  Her steps lead straight to Sheol.†¹

  ⁶ She gives no thought to the way of life.
  Her ways are crooked, and she doesn't know it.

  ⁷ Now therefore, my sons, listen to me.
  Don't depart from the words of my mouth.

  ⁸ Remove your way far from her.
  Don't come near the door of her house,

  ⁹ lest you give your honor to others,
  and your years to the cruel one;

  ¹⁰ lest strangers feast on your wealth,
  and your labors enrich another man's house.

  ¹¹ You will groan at your latter end,

---

when your flesh and your body are consumed,

12 and say, "How I have hated instruction,
and my heart despised reproof.

13 I haven't obeyed the voice of my teachers,
nor turned my ear to those who instructed me!

14 I have come to the brink of utter ruin,
among the gathered assembly."

15 Drink water out of your own cistern,
running water out of your own well.

16 Should your springs overflow in the streets,
streams of water in the public squares?

17 Let them be for yourself alone,
not for strangers with you.

18 Let your spring be blessed.
Rejoice in the wife of your youth.

19 A loving doe and a graceful deer—
let her breasts satisfy you at all times.
Be captivated always with her love.

20 For why should you, my son, be captivated with an adulteress?
Why embrace the bosom of another?

21 For the ways of man are before Yahweh's eyes.
He examines all his paths.

22 The evil deeds of the wicked ensnare him.
The cords of his sin hold him firmly.

23 He will die for lack of instruction.
In the greatness of his folly, he will go astray.

Day 5 – Whispers

Proverbs 5 — Don't Sip the Sweet Poison

> *"For the lips of an adulteress drip honey. Her mouth is smoother than oil, but in the end she is as bitter as wormwood, and as sharp as a two-edged sword."*

> *— Proverbs 5:3–4 (WEB)*

Reflection:

Whew. This one's got bite, doesn't it?
Not every sweetness is safe.
Not every yes is a blessing.
Some things come wrapped in charm and dipped in danger.
Discernment is knowing when something is too sweet to be sincere.
It's tasting the truth beneath the sugar.
It's asking, "Does this build me... or break me slowly?"
Foolishness wears lipstick.
Temptation can sound like affirmation.
But peace? Peace never asks you to betray yourself to get it.
So sip slow. Listen deep.
And don't confuse smooth talk for sound wisdom.
Selah.

Sunrise: Move With Intention

Don't move just to move. Move like something sacred is guiding you.
She says no without guilt. That's divine direction.

He walks slow—but straight. There's power in pacing yourself.

They pause before they leap. Because reflection is a form of power.

Every yes costs something. Spend it wisely.

Today, don't let the world set your rhythm. Let your soul set your pace. Walk with wisdom—and a little sway.

Sunset: Stillness Is Strategy

She sits still and lets the world spin without her. That's not laziness—that's liberation.

He learned: the more still you become, the clearer things speak.

They stopped chasing answers. And the truth walked in.

Stillness is how power gathers its breath.

Let stillness shape your next move. Don't rush the magic.

You don't have to do anything else tonight. You've already done enough. Let your breath be your prayer. Let your stillness be your strength.

Proverbs 6

1 My son, if you have become collateral for your neighbor,
  if you have struck your hands in pledge for a stranger,
  2 you are trapped by the words of your mouth;
  you are ensnared with the words of your mouth.
  3 Do this now, my son, and deliver yourself,
  since you have come into the hand of your neighbor.
  Go, humble yourself.
  Press your plea with your neighbor.
  4 Give no sleep to your eyes,
  nor slumber to your eyelids.
  5 Free yourself, like a gazelle from the hand of the hunter,
  like a bird from the snare of the fowler.
  6 Go to the ant, you sluggard.
  Consider her ways, and be wise;
  7 which having no chief, overseer, or ruler,
  8 provides her bread in the summer,
  and gathers her food in the harvest.
  9 How long will you sleep, sluggard?
  When will you arise out of your sleep?
  10 A little sleep, a little slumber,
  a little folding of the hands to sleep—
  11 so your poverty will come as a robber,
  and your scarcity as an armed man.
  12 A worthless person, a man of iniquity,
  is he who walks with a perverse mouth,
  13 who winks with his eyes, who signals with his feet,

who motions with his fingers,
14 in whose heart is perverseness,
who devises evil continually,
who always sows discord.
15 Therefore his calamity will come suddenly.
He will be broken suddenly, and that without remedy.
16 There are six things which Yahweh hates;
yes, seven which are an abomination to him:
17 arrogant eyes, a lying tongue,
hands that shed innocent blood,
18 a heart that devises wicked schemes,
feet that are swift in running to mischief,
19 a false witness who utters lies,
and he who sows discord among brothers.
20 My son, keep your father's commandment,
and don't forsake your mother's teaching.
21 Bind them continually on your heart.
Tie them around your neck.
22 When you walk, it will lead you.
When you sleep, it will watch over you.
When you awake, it will talk with you.
23 For the commandment is a lamp,
and the law is light.
Reproofs of instruction are the way of life,
24 to keep you from the immoral woman,
from the flattery of the wayward wife's tongue.
25 Don't lust after her beauty in your heart,
neither let her captivate you with her eyelids.
26 For a prostitute reduces you to a piece of bread.
The adulteress hunts for your precious life.
27 Can a man scoop fire into his lap,
and his clothes not be burned?
28 Or can one walk on hot coals,
and his feet not be scorched?
29 So is he who goes in to his neighbor's wife.

Whoever touches her will not be unpunished.

30 Men don't despise a thief

if he steals to satisfy himself when he is hungry,

31 but if he is found, he shall restore seven times.

He shall give all the wealth of his house.

32 He who commits adultery with a woman is void of understanding.

He who does it destroys his own soul.

33 He will get wounds and dishonor.

His reproach will not be wiped away.

34 For jealousy arouses the fury of the husband.

He won't spare in the day of vengeance.

35 He won't regard any ransom,

neither will he rest content, though you give many gifts.

Day 6 – Whispers

Proverbs 6 — Don't Cosign Chaos

> *"My son, if you have become collateral for your neighbor, if you have struck your hands in pledge for a stranger, you are trapped by the words of your mouth..."*
>
> *— Proverbs 6:1–2 (WEB)*

Reflection:

Be careful what you say yes to with your mouth
 Before your heart checks the fine print.
 Not all "help" is holy.
 Not all commitments are covered by purpose.
 Sometimes love looks like *no*.
 Sometimes faith looks like holding your peace.
 Because saying yes to what ain't yours
 Can make you responsible for somebody else's recklessness.
 You ain't here to cosign chaos.
 Be generous, yes—but be wise.
 Because your name carries weight, and your word is your witness.
 Selah.

Sunrise: You Are Not Behind

The timeline you're chasing? Whose is it, really?
 She blooms when she's ready. Not a moment sooner.

He sees folks rushing and smiles. He knows the marathon ain't about the crowd.

They turned comparison into compassion. And peace followed close behind.

You are not behind. You are becoming. Let it take the time it takes.

There is no clock on your calling. No deadline on your destiny. You are unfolding, baby—and it's beautiful.

Sunset: You Are Not Alone

She cried in the dark and still rose with light. She wasn't alone.

He felt invisible—but grace saw him anyway.

They reached out and someone reached back. Divine timing don't miss.

Loneliness is loud. But love whispers through closed doors.

You are held. You are seen. You are loved. Always.

You don't walk this road alone—not now, not ever.

Proverbs 7

1 My son, keep my words.
Lay up my commandments within you.
2 Keep my commandments and live!
Guard my teaching as the apple of your eye.
3 Bind them on your fingers.
Write them on the tablet of your heart.
4 Tell wisdom, "You are my sister."
Call understanding your relative,
5 that they may keep you from the strange woman,
from the foreigner who flatters with her words.
6 For at the window of my house,
I looked out through my lattice.
7 I saw among the simple ones.
I discerned among the youths a young man void of understanding,
8 passing through the street near her corner,
he went the way to her house,
9 in the twilight, in the evening of the day,
in the middle of the night and in the darkness.
10 Behold, there a woman met him with the attire of a prostitute,
and with crafty intent.
11 She is loud and defiant.
Her feet don't stay in her house.
12 Now she is in the streets, now in the squares,
and lurking at every corner.
13 So she caught him, and kissed him.
With an impudent face she said to him:

14 "Sacrifices of peace offerings are with me.
Today I have paid my vows.
15 Therefore I came out to meet you,
to diligently seek your face,
and I have found you.
16 I have spread my couch with carpets of tapestry,
with striped cloths of the yarn of Egypt.
17 I have perfumed my bed with myrrh, aloes, and cinnamon.
18 Come, let's take our fill of loving until the morning.
Let's solace ourselves with loving.
19 For my husband isn't at home.
He has gone on a long journey.
20 He has taken a bag of money with him.
He will come home at the full moon."
21 With persuasive words, she led him astray.
With the flattering of her lips, she seduced him.
22 He followed her immediately,
as an ox goes to the slaughter,
as a fool stepping into a noose.
23 Until an arrow strikes through his liver,
as a bird hurries to the snare,
and doesn't know that it will cost his life.
24 Now therefore, sons, listen to me.
Pay attention to the words of my mouth.
25 Don't let your heart turn to her ways.
Don't go astray in her paths,
26 for she has thrown down many wounded.
Yes, all her slain are a mighty army.
27 Her house is the way to Sheol,†[1]
going down to the rooms of death.

Day 7 – Whispers

Proverbs 7 — Don't Be Wooed by the Wrong Wind

"With persuasive words, she led him astray. She seduced him with her smooth talk. He followed her immediately..."

— Proverbs 7:21–22 (WEB)

Reflection:

Not everything that feels good is *good*.

Charm is cheap when it ain't connected to character.

And smooth talk can steer you straight into soul confusion.

Discernment isn't suspicion—it's sacred wisdom.

It's knowing the difference between real connection and dangerous comfort.

Between purpose and persuasion.

Don't let your need for affirmation

Make you easy prey for performance.

Everything seductive ain't sacred.

Everything flattering ain't for you.

Let peace—not pretty words—lead the way.

Selah.

Sunrise: You Are Already Whole

She stopped chasing perfection. She realized she was already enough.

He dropped the mask. And found freedom in his flaws.

They stood in the mirror and said: "I'm not broken." And meant it.

You don't have to prove your worth. You woke up worthy.

You are already whole. Act like it.

Walk into this day like your soul's been kissed. Because it has. You're not missing pieces—you are the masterpiece.

Sunset: You Are Already Home

She lit a candle and found herself in the glow.

He closed the door and remembered who he was.

They curled into the quiet and felt Spirit settle beside them.

Home is not a place. It's a permission slip to rest.

You are already home. Even if it's just inside yourself.

You don't have to keep looking, striving, seeking. You are home now. Rest in that truth.

Proverbs 8

1 Doesn't wisdom cry out?
Doesn't understanding raise her voice?
2 On the top of high places by the way,
where the paths meet, she stands.
3 Beside the gates, at the entry of the city,
at the entry doors, she cries aloud:
4 "I call to you men!
I send my voice to the sons of mankind.
5 You simple, understand prudence!
You fools, be of an understanding heart!
6 Hear, for I will speak excellent things.
The opening of my lips is for right things.
7 For my mouth speaks truth.
Wickedness is an abomination to my lips.
8 All the words of my mouth are in righteousness.
There is nothing crooked or perverse in them.
9 They are all plain to him who understands,
right to those who find knowledge.
10 Receive my instruction rather than silver,
knowledge rather than choice gold.
11 For wisdom is better than rubies.
All the things that may be desired can't be compared to it.
12 "I, wisdom, have made prudence my dwelling.
Find out knowledge and discretion.
13 The fear of Yahweh is to hate evil.
I hate pride, arrogance, the evil way, and the perverse mouth.

14 Counsel and sound knowledge are mine.
I have understanding and power.
15 By me kings reign,
and princes decree justice.
16 By me princes rule,
nobles, and all the righteous rulers of the earth.
17 I love those who love me.
Those who seek me diligently will find me.
18 With me are riches, honor,
enduring wealth, and prosperity.
19 My fruit is better than gold, yes, than fine gold,
my yield than choice silver.
20 I walk in the way of righteousness,
in the middle of the paths of justice,
21 that I may give wealth to those who love me.
I fill their treasuries.
22 "Yahweh possessed me in the beginning of his work,
before his deeds of old.
23 I was set up from everlasting, from the beginning,
before the earth existed.
24 When there were no depths, I was born,
when there were no springs abounding with water.
25 Before the mountains were settled in place,
before the hills, I was born;
26 while as yet he had not made the earth, nor the fields,
nor the beginning of the dust of the world.
27 When he established the heavens, I was there.
When he set a circle on the surface of the deep,
28 when he established the clouds above,
when the springs of the deep became strong,
29 when he gave to the sea its boundary,
that the waters should not violate his commandment,
when he marked out the foundations of the earth,
30 then I was the craftsman by his side.
I was a delight day by day,

always rejoicing before him,
31 rejoicing in his whole world.
My delight was with the sons of men.
32 "Now therefore, my sons, listen to me,
for blessed are those who keep my ways.
33 Hear instruction, and be wise.
Don't refuse it.
34 Blessed is the man who hears me,
watching daily at my gates,
waiting at my door posts.
35 For whoever finds me finds life,
and will obtain favor from Yahweh.
36 But he who sins against me wrongs his own soul.
All those who hate me love death."

Day 8 – Whispers

Proverbs 8 — Wisdom Is a Woman on the Mic

"Doesn't wisdom cry out? Doesn't understanding raise her voice?"
— Proverbs 8:1 (WEB)

Reflection:

She ain't quiet. She ain't shy.
    Wisdom is a woman with a bullhorn on the block,
    Calling your name before you step too far.
    She stands at every crossroad.
    She's louder than the lie.
    But you gotta tune your ears to her frequency.
    Don't say God ain't speaking
    When you've been hitting "mute" on everything that don't flatter you.
    Wisdom's voice isn't always sweet—
    But it's saving you even when it stings.
    So listen. Loud and deep.
    She's already speaking. You just gotta want to hear.
    Selah.

Sunrise: Boundaries Are a Blessing

She said "no" with love. That was her freedom song.
　　He didn't explain his boundary. He just built it.
　　They made space for peace. And peace showed up.
　　Every yes that honors you is a holy thing.
　　Boundaries are a blessing. For you. For them. For growth.
　　Move through today like your time is sacred—because it is.

Sunset: Protect Your Peace

She chose silence over the last word. Peace won.
　　He shut the screen, lit a candle, and came back to himself.
　　They left the chat. Spirit stayed online.
　　Not every battle deserves your brilliance.
　　Protect your peace like it pays your bills. 'Cause it kinda does.
　　You don't need to argue to exist. Just breathe, baby. You're doing fine.

Proverbs 9

1 Wisdom has built her house.
  She has carved out her seven pillars.
  2 She has prepared her meat.
  She has mixed her wine.
  She has also set her table.
  3 She has sent out her maidens.
  She cries from the highest places of the city:
  4 "Whoever is simple, let him turn in here!"
  As for him who is void of understanding, she says to him,
  5 "Come, eat some of my bread,
  Drink some of the wine which I have mixed!
  6 Leave your simple ways, and live.
  Walk in the way of understanding."
  7 One who corrects a mocker invites insult.
  One who reproves a wicked man invites abuse.
  8 Don't reprove a scoffer, lest he hate you.
  Reprove a wise person, and he will love you.
  9 Instruct a wise person, and he will be still wiser.
  Teach a righteous person, and he will increase in learning.
  10 The fear of Yahweh is the beginning of wisdom.
  The knowledge of the Holy One is understanding.
  11 For by me your days will be multiplied.
  The years of your life will be increased.
  12 If you are wise, you are wise for yourself.
  If you mock, you alone will bear it.
  13 The foolish woman is loud,

undisciplined, and knows nothing.
14 She sits at the door of her house,
on a seat in the high places of the city,
15 to call to those who pass by,
who go straight on their ways,
16 "Whoever is simple, let him turn in here."
As for him who is void of understanding, she says to him,
17 "Stolen water is sweet.
Food eaten in secret is pleasant."
18 But he doesn't know that the departed spirits are there,
that her guests are in the depths of Sheol.†

Day 9 – Whispers

Proverbs 9 — Both Wisdom and Foolishness Set the Table

"Wisdom has built her house... she has prepared her meat... she calls from the highest places... The foolish woman is loud... she sits at the door... and calls to those who pass by."

— Proverbs 9:1-3, 13–15 (WEB)

Reflection:

Two invitations.
Two voices.
Both dressed in welcome. Only one ends in life.
Foolishness be flashy.
She's loud and lazy, just waiting to pull you in.
But Wisdom? She built something. She prepared something.
She earned the right to feed you.
The difference?
One fills your belly. The other steals your future.
So check the table before you sit.
And ask—was this made with love or with illusion?
Because both are calling. But only one is real food.
Selah.

Sunrise: Trust the Unseen

She trusted what hadn't bloomed yet. Faith watered it daily.

He walked blind—but guided.

They stopped needing proof to have peace.

Let the unknown be a soft place, not a scary one.

Trust the unseen. It sees you.

Your next chapter already knows your name. Trust that. Now go be brilliant anyway.

<u>Sunset: Let It Go Before Bed</u>

She released what wasn't hers to carry. And slept deeper than she had in weeks.

He forgave what would never be fixed. Not for them—for his own peace.

They cried a little. Then smiled a lot.

Some chapters don't need closure. Just a period.

Let it go. Breathe. Heal in your sleep.

You don't need to solve it tonight. You just need to rest.

Proverbs 10

1 The proverbs of Solomon.

A wise son makes a glad father;
but a foolish son brings grief to his mother.
2 Treasures of wickedness profit nothing,
but righteousness delivers from death.
3 Yahweh will not allow the soul of the righteous to go hungry,
but he thrusts away the desire of the wicked.
4 He becomes poor who works with a lazy hand,
but the hand of the diligent brings wealth.
5 He who gathers in summer is a wise son,
but he who sleeps during the harvest is a son who causes shame.
6 Blessings are on the head of the righteous,
but violence covers the mouth of the wicked.
7 The memory of the righteous is blessed,
but the name of the wicked will rot.
8 The wise in heart accept commandments,
but a chattering fool will fall.
9 He who walks blamelessly walks surely,
but he who perverts his ways will be found out.
10 One who winks with the eye causes sorrow,
but a chattering fool will fall.
11 The mouth of the righteous is a spring of life,
but violence covers the mouth of the wicked.
12 Hatred stirs up strife,
but love covers all wrongs.
13 Wisdom is found on the lips of him who has discernment,

but a rod is for the back of him who is void of understanding.
14 Wise men lay up knowledge,
but the mouth of the foolish is near ruin.
15 The rich man's wealth is his strong city.
The destruction of the poor is their poverty.
16 The labor of the righteous leads to life.
The increase of the wicked leads to sin.
17 He is in the way of life who heeds correction,
but he who forsakes reproof leads others astray.
18 He who hides hatred has lying lips.
He who utters a slander is a fool.
19 In the multitude of words there is no lack of disobedience,
but he who restrains his lips does wisely.
20 The tongue of the righteous is like choice silver.
The heart of the wicked is of little worth.
21 The lips of the righteous feed many,
but the foolish die for lack of understanding.
22 Yahweh's blessing brings wealth,
and he adds no trouble to it.
23 It is a fool's pleasure to do wickedness,
but wisdom is a man of understanding's pleasure.
24 What the wicked fear will overtake them,
but the desire of the righteous will be granted.
25 When the whirlwind passes, the wicked is no more;
but the righteous stand firm forever.
26 As vinegar to the teeth, and as smoke to the eyes,
so is the sluggard to those who send him.
27 The fear of Yahweh prolongs days,
but the years of the wicked shall be shortened.
28 The prospect of the righteous is joy,
but the hope of the wicked will perish.
29 The way of Yahweh is a stronghold to the upright,
but it is a destruction to the workers of iniquity.
30 The righteous will never be removed,
but the wicked will not dwell in the land.

31 The mouth of the righteous produces wisdom,
but the perverse tongue will be cut off.
32 The lips of the righteous know what is acceptable,
but the mouth of the wicked is perverse.

Day 10 – Whispers

Proverbs 10 — Your Mouth Makes the Weather

"The mouth of the righteous is a spring of life... The lips of the righteous feed many..."

— Proverbs 10:11, 21 (WEB)

Reflection:

What comes out your mouth? Rain or fire?
    Nourishment or noise?
    Your words plant seeds—
    And what you sow will grow.
    Speak slow.
    Bless bold.
    Know when silence is the best sermon.
    A righteous mouth ain't just about holiness—
    It's about healing. It's about knowing your tongue is a tool, not a toy.
    So speak life. Speak peace.
    And if you ain't sure—sip some wisdom first.
    Selah.

Sunrise: Courage Looks Good on You

She did it scared. And did it well.

He stood in his truth—even when his voice shook.

They weren't fearless. They were faithful.

Courage isn't loud. Sometimes it whispers, "Try again."

Courage looks good on you. Go shine.

Be the most you you've ever been. You got this.

Sunset: Rest Like You're Brave

She laid it all down. Even the things she loved—but needed to leave.

He turned off the world. And tuned into himself.

They slept like they trusted the future. And woke up free.

Bravery is choosing peace when chaos feels familiar.

Rest like you're brave. Because you are.

Even fighters need sleep. And tomorrow? It'll meet you with joy.

Proverbs 11

1 A false balance is an abomination to Yahweh,
   but accurate weights are his delight.
2 When pride comes, then comes shame,
   but with humility comes wisdom.
3 The integrity of the upright shall guide them,
   but the perverseness of the treacherous shall destroy them.
4 Riches don't profit in the day of wrath,
   but righteousness delivers from death.
5 The righteousness of the blameless will direct his way,
   but the wicked shall fall by his own wickedness.
6 The righteousness of the upright shall deliver them,
   but the unfaithful will be trapped by evil desires.
7 When a wicked man dies, hope perishes,
   and expectation of power comes to nothing.
8 A righteous person is delivered out of trouble,
   and the wicked takes his place.
9 With his mouth the godless man destroys his neighbor,
   but the righteous will be delivered through knowledge.
10 When it goes well with the righteous, the city rejoices.
   When the wicked perish, there is shouting.
11 By the blessing of the upright, the city is exalted,
   but it is overthrown by the mouth of the wicked.
12 One who despises his neighbor is void of wisdom,
   but a man of understanding holds his peace.
13 One who brings gossip betrays a confidence,
   but one who is of a trustworthy spirit is one who keeps a secret.

14 Where there is no wise guidance, the nation falls,
but in the multitude of counselors there is victory.
15 He who is collateral for a stranger will suffer for it,
but he who refuses pledges of collateral is secure.
16 A gracious woman obtains honor,
but violent men obtain riches.
17 The merciful man does good to his own soul,
but he who is cruel troubles his own flesh.
18 Wicked people earn deceitful wages,
but one who sows righteousness reaps a sure reward.
19 He who is truly righteous gets life.
He who pursues evil gets death.
20 Those who are perverse in heart are an abomination to Yahweh,
but those whose ways are blameless are his delight.
21 Most certainly, the evil man will not be unpunished,
but the offspring† of the righteous will be delivered.
22 Like a gold ring in a pig's snout,
is a beautiful woman who lacks discretion.
23 The desire of the righteous is only good.
The expectation of the wicked is wrath.
24 There is one who scatters, and increases yet more.
There is one who withholds more than is appropriate, but gains poverty.
25 The liberal soul shall be made fat.
He who waters shall be watered also himself.
26 People curse someone who withholds grain,
but blessing will be on the head of him who sells it.
27 He who diligently seeks good seeks favor,
but he who searches after evil, it shall come to him.
28 He who trusts in his riches will fall,
but the righteous shall flourish as the green leaf.
29 He who troubles his own house shall inherit the wind.
The foolish shall be servant to the wise of heart.
30 The fruit of the righteous is a tree of life.
He who is wise wins souls.
31 Behold, the righteous shall be repaid in the earth,

how much more the wicked and the sinner!

Day 11 – Whispers

Proverbs 11 — The Weight of the Scale

"A false balance is an abomination to Yahweh, but accurate weights are his delight."

— Proverbs 11:1 (WEB)

Reflection:

Fairness ain't just for courtrooms.
    God watches how you do business, too.
    How you treat folks when no one's watching.
    How honest your yes really is.
    Integrity is balance.
    Lies tilt the scale for profit, but truth stands steady—unshaken.
    So check your scales, sis.
    Not just in money, but in motive.
    Measure your actions with justice, not ego.
    Because what feels like a shortcut today
    Might just be a soul debt tomorrow.
    Selah.

Sunrise: Joy Is a Rebellion

She laughed before anything was funny. That's how joy found her.
He sang off-key but with full chest. That's how joy stayed.
They danced barefoot in the kitchen. No audience. Just freedom.
Joy doesn't need a reason. Joy is the reason.
Joy is a rebellion. Choose it anyway.

Sunset: Make Room for Joy

She opened her window and let laughter in.
He turned the music up, even though it was late.
They smiled in the dark. Because joy don't need daylight.
Joy can live here, even with the pain.
Make room for joy. Even if it's just a crack.

Proverbs 12

1 Whoever loves correction loves knowledge,
   but he who hates reproof is stupid.
   2 A good man shall obtain favor from Yahweh,
   but he will condemn a man of wicked plans.
   3 A man shall not be established by wickedness,
   but the root of the righteous shall not be moved.
   4 A worthy woman is the crown of her husband,
   but a disgraceful wife is as rottenness in his bones.
   5 The thoughts of the righteous are just,
   but the advice of the wicked is deceitful.
   6 The words of the wicked are about lying in wait for blood,
   but the speech of the upright rescues them.
   7 The wicked are overthrown, and are no more,
   but the house of the righteous shall stand.
   8 A man shall be commended according to his wisdom,
   but he who has a warped mind shall be despised.
   9 Better is he who is little known, and has a servant,
   than he who honors himself and lacks bread.
   10 A righteous man respects the life of his animal,
   but the tender mercies of the wicked are cruel.
   11 He who tills his land shall have plenty of bread,
   but he who chases fantasies is void of understanding.
   12 The wicked desires the plunder of evil men,
   but the root of the righteous flourishes.
   13 An evil man is trapped by sinfulness of lips,
   but the righteous shall come out of trouble.

14 A man shall be satisfied with good by the fruit of his mouth.
The work of a man's hands shall be rewarded to him.
15 The way of a fool is right in his own eyes,
but he who is wise listens to counsel.
16 A fool shows his annoyance the same day,
but one who overlooks an insult is prudent.
17 He who is truthful testifies honestly,
but a false witness lies.
18 There is one who speaks rashly like the piercing of a sword,
but the tongue of the wise heals.
19 Truth's lips will be established forever,
but a lying tongue is only momentary.
20 Deceit is in the heart of those who plot evil,
but joy comes to the promoters of peace.
21 No mischief shall happen to the righteous,
but the wicked shall be filled with evil.
22 Lying lips are an abomination to Yahweh,
but those who do the truth are his delight.
23 A prudent man keeps his knowledge,
but the hearts of fools proclaim foolishness.
24 The hands of the diligent ones shall rule,
but laziness ends in slave labor.
25 Anxiety in a man's heart weighs it down,
but a kind word makes it glad.
26 A righteous person is cautious in friendship,
but the way of the wicked leads them astray.
27 The slothful man doesn't roast his game,
but the possessions of diligent men are prized.
28 In the way of righteousness is life;
in its path there is no death.

Day 12 – Whispers

Proverbs 12 — Work Speaks Louder Than Wishes

"He who tills his land shall have plenty of bread, but he who chases fantasies is void of understanding."

— Proverbs 12:11 (WEB)

Reflection:

Dreams don't grow without dirt under your nails.
 Wishing don't work unless your hands do.
 You can't harvest what you won't hustle for.
 You can't eat from fields you only fantasize about.
 Till the land. Show up daily.
 Let your work be your worship.
 Because faith ain't lazy—it plants, waters, and waits.
 And fantasy without effort?
 That's just procrastination in a pretty dress.
 Selah.

Sunrise: Resilience Is a Rhythm

She got knocked down—and got cuter getting back up.

He didn't rush the bounce-back. He moved with rhythm, not reaction.

They grew roots while the world wasn't watching.

Resilience doesn't mean you don't fall. It means you rise soft, not bitter.

Resilience is a rhythm. Catch the beat.

<u>Sunset: You're Allowed to Rest</u>

She let herself be held—by sleep, by Spirit, by silence.

He stopped pushing for one night—and the sky didn't fall.

They allowed the pause. That's where healing slipped in.

Rest is not quitting. Rest is preparing.

You're allowed to rest. Especially you.

Proverbs 13

1 A wise son listens to his father's instruction,
but a scoffer doesn't listen to rebuke.
2 By the fruit of his lips, a man enjoys good things,
but the unfaithful crave violence.
3 He who guards his mouth guards his soul.
One who opens wide his lips comes to ruin.
4 The soul of the sluggard desires, and has nothing,
but the desire of the diligent shall be fully satisfied.
5 A righteous man hates lies,
but a wicked man brings shame and disgrace.
6 Righteousness guards the way of integrity,
but wickedness overthrows the sinner.
7 There are some who pretend to be rich, yet have nothing.
There are some who pretend to be poor, yet have great wealth.
8 The ransom of a man's life is his riches,
but the poor hear no threats.
9 The light of the righteous shines brightly,
but the lamp of the wicked is snuffed out.
10 Pride only breeds quarrels,
but wisdom is with people who take advice.
11 Wealth gained dishonestly dwindles away,
but he who gathers by hand makes it grow.
12 Hope deferred makes the heart sick,
but when longing is fulfilled, it is a tree of life.
13 Whoever despises instruction will pay for it,
but he who respects a command will be rewarded.

14 The teaching of the wise is a spring of life,
to turn from the snares of death.
15 Good understanding wins favor,
but the way of the unfaithful is hard.
16 Every prudent man acts from knowledge,
but a fool exposes folly.
17 A wicked messenger falls into trouble,
but a trustworthy envoy gains healing.
18 Poverty and shame come to him who refuses discipline,
but he who heeds correction shall be honored.
19 Longing fulfilled is sweet to the soul,
but fools detest turning from evil.
20 One who walks with wise men grows wise,
but a companion of fools suffers harm.
21 Misfortune pursues sinners,
but prosperity rewards the righteous.
22 A good man leaves an inheritance to his children's children,
but the wealth of the sinner is stored for the righteous.
23 An abundance of food is in poor people's fields,
but injustice sweeps it away.
24 One who spares the rod hates his son,
but one who loves him is careful to discipline him.
25 The righteous one eats to the satisfying of his soul,
but the belly of the wicked goes hungry.

Day 13 – Whispers

Proverbs 13 — Walk With the Wise

"One who walks with wise men grows wise, but a companion of fools suffers harm."

— Proverbs 13:20 (WEB)

Reflection:

Your circle is your future.
> Your friends are your forecast.
> You can't run with fools and stay smart.
> Can't keep company with chaos and expect calm.
> Wisdom is contagious—but so is foolishness.
> So audit your people.
> Ask yourself—who sharpens me? Who silences me? Who drains me dry?
> Because who you walk with
> Will shape where you end up.
> Selah.

Sunrise: Let Them Go in Love

She loved them from afar. And let them fly.

He stopped chasing the closed door.

They mourned what never became—and made room for what could.

Letting go isn't failure. It's faith in a future you can't see yet.

Let them go in love. That's how you grow.

Sunset: Don't Chase, Attract

She stopped knocking. The door opened anyway.

He let go of what ran—and watched what stayed.

They focused inward. Everything aligned.

Chasing drains. Attracting renews.

Don't chase. Attract. And rest in that power.

Proverbs 14

1 Every wise woman builds her house,
    but the foolish one tears it down with her own hands.
2 He who walks in his uprightness fears Yahweh,
    but he who is perverse in his ways despises him.
3 The fool's talk brings a rod to his back,
    but the lips of the wise protect them.
4 Where no oxen are, the crib is clean,
    but much increase is by the strength of the ox.
5 A truthful witness will not lie,
    but a false witness pours out lies.
6 A scoffer seeks wisdom, and doesn't find it,
    but knowledge comes easily to a discerning person.
7 Stay away from a foolish man,
    for you won't find knowledge on his lips.
8 The wisdom of the prudent is to think about his way,
    but the folly of fools is deceit.
9 Fools mock at making atonement for sins,
    but among the upright there is good will.
10 The heart knows its own bitterness and joy;
    he will not share these with a stranger.
11 The house of the wicked will be overthrown,
    but the tent of the upright will flourish.
12 There is a way which seems right to a man,
    but in the end it leads to death.
13 Even in laughter the heart may be sorrowful,
    and mirth may end in heaviness.

14 The unfaithful will be repaid for his own ways;
likewise a good man will be rewarded for his ways.
15 A simple man believes everything,
but the prudent man carefully considers his ways.
16 A wise man fears and shuns evil,
but the fool is hot headed and reckless.
17 He who is quick to become angry will commit folly,
and a crafty man is hated.
18 The simple inherit folly,
but the prudent are crowned with knowledge.
19 The evil bow down before the good,
and the wicked at the gates of the righteous.
20 The poor person is shunned even by his own neighbor,
but the rich person has many friends.
21 He who despises his neighbor sins,
but he who has pity on the poor is blessed.
22 Don't they go astray who plot evil?
But love and faithfulness belong to those who plan good.
23 In all hard work there is profit,
but the talk of the lips leads only to poverty.
24 The crown of the wise is their riches,
but the folly of fools crowns them with folly.
25 A truthful witness saves souls,
but a false witness is deceitful.
26 In the fear of Yahweh is a secure fortress,
and he will be a refuge for his children.
27 The fear of Yahweh is a fountain of life,
turning people from the snares of death.
28 In the multitude of people is the king's glory,
but in the lack of people is the destruction of the prince.
29 He who is slow to anger has great understanding,
but he who has a quick temper displays folly.
30 The life of the body is a heart at peace,
but envy rots the bones.
31 He who oppresses the poor shows contempt for his Maker,

but he who is kind to the needy honors him.
32 The wicked is brought down in his calamity,
but in death, the righteous has a refuge.
33 Wisdom rests in the heart of one who has understanding,
and is even made known in the inward part of fools.
34 Righteousness exalts a nation,
but sin is a disgrace to any people.
35 The king's favor is toward a servant who deals wisely,
but his wrath is toward one who causes shame.

Day 14 – Whispers

Proverbs 14 — Quiet Confidence

"In the fear of Yahweh is a secure fortress, and he will be a refuge for his children."

— Proverbs 14:26 (WEB)

Reflection:

Real confidence ain't loud.
　　It don't need applause to stand tall.
　　It's quiet. Rooted. Reverent.
　　Because it knows who holds the fortress.
　　You don't have to flex when you're fortified.
　　You don't have to shout when your source is steady.
　　Let your trust speak for itself.
　　Let your peace preach the sermon.
　　You're covered. You're kept. You're held.
　　Selah.

Sunrise: Talk to Your Inner Child

She told the little girl in her: "You're safe now."

He listened to the younger him—and didn't dismiss his tears.

They made space for joy, not just survival.

Healing the child makes room for the adult to rest.

Talk to your inner child today. They still believe in magic. And so should you.

Sunset: Hold the Child Within

She tucked herself in with kindness—not criticism.

He whispered to his younger self: "You made it."

They forgave the child they once were—for just trying to survive.

Healing isn't loud. Sometimes, it's a bedtime story to yourself.

Hold the child within. They've been waiting to rest.

Proverbs 15

1 A gentle answer turns away wrath,
   but a harsh word stirs up anger.
2 The tongue of the wise commends knowledge,
   but the mouths of fools gush out folly.
3 Yahweh's eyes are everywhere,
   keeping watch on the evil and the good.
4 A gentle tongue is a tree of life,
   but deceit in it crushes the spirit.
5 A fool despises his father's correction,
   but he who heeds reproof shows prudence.
6 In the house of the righteous is much treasure,
   but the income of the wicked brings trouble.
7 The lips of the wise spread knowledge;
   not so with the heart of fools.
8 The sacrifice made by the wicked is an abomination to Yahweh,
   but the prayer of the upright is his delight.
9 The way of the wicked is an abomination to Yahweh,
   but he loves him who follows after righteousness.
10 There is stern discipline for one who forsakes the way.
   Whoever hates reproof shall die.
11 Sheol†[1] and Abaddon are before Yahweh—
   how much more then the hearts of the children of men!
12 A scoffer doesn't love to be reproved;
   he will not go to the wise.
13 A glad heart makes a cheerful face,

---

1.   https://ebible.org/eng-web/PRO15.htm#FN1

but an aching heart breaks the spirit.
14 The heart of one who has understanding seeks knowledge,
but the mouths of fools feed on folly.
15 All the days of the afflicted are wretched,
but one who has a cheerful heart enjoys a continual feast.
16 Better is little, with the fear of Yahweh,
than great treasure with trouble.
17 Better is a dinner of herbs, where love is,
than a fattened calf with hatred.
18 A wrathful man stirs up contention,
but one who is slow to anger appeases strife.
19 The way of the sluggard is like a thorn patch,
but the path of the upright is a highway.
20 A wise son makes a father glad,
but a foolish man despises his mother.
21 Folly is joy to one who is void of wisdom,
but a man of understanding keeps his way straight.
22 Where there is no counsel, plans fail;
but in a multitude of counselors they are established.
23 Joy comes to a man with the reply of his mouth.
How good is a word at the right time!
24 The path of life leads upward for the wise,
to keep him from going downward to Sheol.‡[2]
25 Yahweh will uproot the house of the proud,
but he will keep the widow's borders intact.
26 Yahweh detests the thoughts of the wicked,
but the thoughts of the pure are pleasing.
27 He who is greedy for gain troubles his own house,
but he who hates bribes will live.
28 The heart of the righteous weighs answers,
but the mouth of the wicked gushes out evil.
29 Yahweh is far from the wicked,
but he hears the prayer of the righteous.
30 The light of the eyes rejoices the heart.

2.   https://ebible.org/eng-web/PRO15.htm#FN2

Good news gives health to the bones.
31 The ear that listens to reproof lives,
and will be at home among the wise.
32 He who refuses correction despises his own soul,
but he who listens to reproof gets understanding.
33 The fear of Yahweh teaches wisdom.
Before honor is humility.

Day 15 – Whispers

Proverbs 15 — Soft Wins

"A gentle answer turns away wrath, but a harsh word stirs up anger."
— Proverbs 15:1 (WEB)

Reflection:

Soft don't mean weak.

    It means wise enough to know when to lower the volume.

    Some battles are won with silence.

    Some with a smile.

    Some with a soft word that disarms the dagger.

    Every raised voice don't deserve an echo.

    And every insult ain't worth your energy.

    Power is knowing when peace is the louder answer.

    Selah.

Sunrise: Softness Is Not Weakness

She cried—and then got up. That's strength.
　　He led with tenderness, not toughness.
　　They let softness soften the world around them.
　　Your strength doesn't have to be loud to be real.
　　Softness is not weakness. It's wisdom wrapped in velvet.

<u>Sunset: Lay Down the Armor</u>

She removed her armor and exhaled.
　　He set his sword aside—and picked up peace.
　　They stopped proving. Started resting.
　　Every strong one deserves a soft place to land.
　　Lay down the armor tonight. Your spirit needs a hug, not a battle.

Proverbs 16

1 The plans of the heart belong to man,
 but the answer of the tongue is from Yahweh.
2 All the ways of a man are clean in his own eyes,
 but Yahweh weighs the motives.
3 Commit your deeds to Yahweh,
 and your plans shall succeed.
4 Yahweh has made everything for its own end—
 yes, even the wicked for the day of evil.
5 Everyone who is proud in heart is an abomination to Yahweh;
 they shall certainly not be unpunished.
6 By mercy and truth iniquity is atoned for.
 By the fear of Yahweh men depart from evil.
7 When a man's ways please Yahweh,
 he makes even his enemies to be at peace with him.
8 Better is a little with righteousness,
 than great revenues with injustice.
9 A man's heart plans his course,
 but Yahweh directs his steps.
10 Inspired judgments are on the lips of the king.
 He shall not betray his mouth.
11 Honest balances and scales are Yahweh's;
 all the weights in the bag are his work.
12 It is an abomination for kings to do wrong,
 for the throne is established by righteousness.
13 Righteous lips are the delight of kings.
 They value one who speaks the truth.

14 The king's wrath is a messenger of death,
but a wise man will pacify it.
15 In the light of the king's face is life.
His favor is like a cloud of the spring rain.
16 How much better it is to get wisdom than gold!
Yes, to get understanding is to be chosen rather than silver.
17 The highway of the upright is to depart from evil.
He who keeps his way preserves his soul.
18 Pride goes before destruction,
and an arrogant spirit before a fall.
19 It is better to be of a lowly spirit with the poor,
than to divide the plunder with the proud.
20 He who heeds the Word finds prosperity.
Whoever trusts in Yahweh is blessed.
21 The wise in heart shall be called prudent.
Pleasantness of the lips promotes instruction.
22 Understanding is a fountain of life to one who has it,
but the punishment of fools is their folly.
23 The heart of the wise instructs his mouth,
and adds learning to his lips.
24 Pleasant words are a honeycomb,
sweet to the soul, and health to the bones.
25 There is a way which seems right to a man,
but in the end it leads to death.
26 The appetite of the laboring man labors for him,
for his mouth urges him on.
27 A worthless man devises mischief.
His speech is like a scorching fire.
28 A perverse man stirs up strife.
A whisperer separates close friends.
29 A man of violence entices his neighbor,
and leads him in a way that is not good.
30 One who winks his eyes to plot perversities,
one who compresses his lips, is bent on evil.
31 Gray hair is a crown of glory.

It is attained by a life of righteousness.
32 One who is slow to anger is better than the mighty;
one who rules his spirit, than he who takes a city.
33 The lot is cast into the lap,
but its every decision is from Yahweh.

Day 16 – Whispers

Proverbs 16 — God Got the GPS

"A man's heart plans his course, but Yahweh directs his steps."
— Proverbs 16:9 (WEB)

Reflection:

You might map it all out—vision board, 5-year plan, color-coded calendar.
　　But at the end of the day?
　　God holds the highlighter.
　　You're not off course just because the route changed.
　　Sometimes detours *are* divine.
　　And every closed door isn't rejection—it might just be redirection.
　　Keep planning. Keep dreaming.
　　But hold your steps loosely,
　　So God can reroute you with grace, not struggle.
　　The destination's still yours.
　　But trust the One with the map.
　　Selah.

Sunrise: Your Ancestors Walk With You

She heard her grandmother's prayers in her heartbeat.

He walked into the courtroom like his granddaddy walked into battle.

They don't walk alone. Legacy holds their hand.

You carry their names, their dreams, their fire.

Your ancestors walk with you. Every step is sacred.

Sunset: Say Thank You to Those Who Came Before

She whispered, "Thank you," to the ones whose names she never knew.

He poured libations in his mind, and in his rest.

They lit candles with memory in their flame.

The ancestors rejoice when you rest.

Say thank you. Then sleep like you've been chosen.

Proverbs 17

1 Better is a dry morsel with quietness,
  than a house full of feasting with strife.
2 A servant who deals wisely will rule over a son who causes shame,
  and shall have a part in the inheritance among the brothers.
3 The refining pot is for silver, and the furnace for gold,
  but Yahweh tests the hearts.
4 An evildoer heeds wicked lips.
  A liar gives ear to a mischievous tongue.
5 Whoever mocks the poor reproaches his Maker.
  He who is glad at calamity shall not be unpunished.
6 Children's children are the crown of old men;
  the glory of children is their parents.
7 Excellent speech isn't fitting for a fool,
  much less do lying lips fit a prince.
8 A bribe is a precious stone in the eyes of him who gives it;
  wherever he turns, he prospers.
9 He who covers an offense promotes love;
  but he who repeats a matter separates best friends.
10 A rebuke enters deeper into one who has understanding
  than a hundred lashes into a fool.
11 An evil man seeks only rebellion;
  therefore a cruel messenger shall be sent against him.
12 Let a bear robbed of her cubs meet a man,
  rather than a fool in his folly.
13 Whoever rewards evil for good,
  evil shall not depart from his house.

14 The beginning of strife is like breaching a dam,
therefore stop contention before quarreling breaks out.
15 He who justifies the wicked, and he who condemns the righteous,
both of them alike are an abomination to Yahweh.
16 Why is there money in the hand of a fool to buy wisdom,
since he has no understanding?
17 A friend loves at all times;
and a brother is born for adversity.
18 A man void of understanding strikes hands,
and becomes collateral in the presence of his neighbor.
19 He who loves disobedience loves strife.
One who builds a high gate seeks destruction.
20 One who has a perverse heart doesn't find prosperity,
and one who has a deceitful tongue falls into trouble.
21 He who becomes the father of a fool grieves.
The father of a fool has no joy.
22 A cheerful heart makes good medicine,
but a crushed spirit dries up the bones.
23 A wicked man receives a bribe in secret,
to pervert the ways of justice.
24 Wisdom is before the face of one who has understanding,
but the eyes of a fool wander to the ends of the earth.
25 A foolish son brings grief to his father,
and bitterness to her who bore him.
26 Also to punish the righteous is not good,
nor to flog officials for their integrity.
27 He who spares his words has knowledge.
He who is even tempered is a man of understanding.
28 Even a fool, when he keeps silent, is counted wise.
When he shuts his lips, he is thought to be discerning.

Day 17 – Whispers

Proverbs 17 — Quiet is a Flex

"Even a fool, when he keeps silent, is counted wise. When he shuts his lips, he is thought to be discerning."

— Proverbs 17:28 (WEB)

Reflection:

You don't always have to clap back.
    You don't always have to explain.
    Sometimes silence is the wisest sentence you'll ever write.
    Let 'em talk. Let 'em twist it. Let 'em wonder.
    Because wisdom knows when to hush
    And let peace speak for her.
    If folks confuse your stillness for weakness,
    Let them.
    You ain't here to be understood by everybody.
    You're here to stay grounded in your knowing.
    Selah.

Sunrise: Forgiveness Is for You Too

She forgave herself for not knowing back then what she knows now.
He dropped the grudge—not to forget, but to be free.
They released bitterness like breath. One exhale at a time.
Forgiveness isn't about them. It's medicine for you.
Forgiveness is for you too. Take the dose.

Sunset: Rest Without Regret

She stopped the replay and pressed pause.
He made peace with the messy middle.
They closed the chapter with a whisper, not a scream.
You can sleep soft—even if today wasn't perfect.
Rest without regret. Tomorrow don't need your guilt.

Proverbs 18

1 A man who isolates himself pursues selfishness,
and defies all sound judgment.
2 A fool has no delight in understanding,
but only in revealing his own opinion.
3 When wickedness comes, contempt also comes,
and with shame comes disgrace.
4 The words of a man's mouth are like deep waters.
The fountain of wisdom is like a flowing brook.
5 To be partial to the faces of the wicked is not good,
nor to deprive the innocent of justice.
6 A fool's lips come into strife,
and his mouth invites beatings.
7 A fool's mouth is his destruction,
and his lips are a snare to his soul.
8 The words of a gossip are like dainty morsels:
they go down into a person's innermost parts.
9 One who is slack in his work
is brother to him who is a master of destruction.
10 Yahweh's name is a strong tower:
the righteous run to him, and are safe.
11 The rich man's wealth is his strong city,
like an unscalable wall in his own imagination.
12 Before destruction the heart of man is proud,
but before honor is humility.
13 He who answers before he hears,
that is folly and shame to him.

14 A man's spirit will sustain him in sickness,
but a crushed spirit, who can bear?
15 The heart of the discerning gets knowledge.
The ear of the wise seeks knowledge.
16 A man's gift makes room for him,
and brings him before great men.
17 He who pleads his cause first seems right—
until another comes and questions him.
18 The lot settles disputes,
and keeps strong ones apart.
19 A brother offended is more difficult than a fortified city.
Disputes are like the bars of a fortress.
20 A man's stomach is filled with the fruit of his mouth.
With the harvest of his lips he is satisfied.
21 Death and life are in the power of the tongue;
those who love it will eat its fruit.
22 Whoever finds a wife finds a good thing,
and obtains favor of Yahweh.
23 The poor plead for mercy,
but the rich answer harshly.
24 A man of many companions may be ruined,
but there is a friend who sticks closer than a brother.

Day 18 – Whispers

Proverbs 18 — Life or Death on Your Tongue

"Death and life are in the power of the tongue; those who love it will eat its fruit."

— Proverbs 18:21 (WEB)

Reflection:

Your mouth is a garden and a battlefield.
Every word you speak grows something.
Bitterness or beauty.
Breakdown or blessing.
Speak slow.
Speak true.
Speak with the weight of eternity tucked behind your teeth.
Because once a word flies,
You can't pull it back into your mouth like it didn't happen.
So plant wisely.
Water gently.
And only harvest what you're ready to eat.
Selah.

Sunrise: Confidence Can Be Quiet

She didn't argue. She just adjusted her crown and moved on.
　He didn't need applause to feel proud.
　They didn't shrink or shout. They showed up steady.
　Confidence isn't always loud. Sometimes it whispers, "Watch me work."
　Confidence can be quiet. And still shake the room.

Sunset: No Need to Prove Yourself

She didn't chase validation. She invited peace.
　He let his work speak. Then stayed silent.
　They unplugged from the pressure to perform.
　You're not for everyone. That's freedom, not failure.
　You don't have to prove yourself. Just be yourself.

Proverbs 19

1 Better is the poor who walks in his integrity
   than he who is perverse in his lips and is a fool.
2 It isn't good to have zeal without knowledge,
   nor being hasty with one's feet and missing the way.
3 The foolishness of man subverts his way;
   his heart rages against Yahweh.
4 Wealth adds many friends,
   but the poor is separated from his friend.
5 A false witness shall not be unpunished.
   He who pours out lies shall not go free.
6 Many will entreat the favor of a ruler,
   and everyone is a friend to a man who gives gifts.
7 All the relatives of the poor shun him;
   how much more do his friends avoid him!
   He pursues them with pleas, but they are gone.
8 He who gets wisdom loves his own soul.
   He who keeps understanding shall find good.
9 A false witness shall not be unpunished.
   He who utters lies shall perish.
10 Delicate living is not appropriate for a fool,
   much less for a servant to have rule over princes.
11 The discretion of a man makes him slow to anger.
   It is his glory to overlook an offense.
12 The king's wrath is like the roaring of a lion,
   but his favor is like dew on the grass.
13 A foolish son is the calamity of his father.

A wife's quarrels are a continual dripping.
14 House and riches are an inheritance from fathers,
but a prudent wife is from Yahweh.
15 Slothfulness casts into a deep sleep.
The idle soul shall suffer hunger.
16 He who keeps the commandment keeps his soul,
but he who is contemptuous in his ways shall die.
17 He who has pity on the poor lends to Yahweh;
he will reward him.
18 Discipline your son, for there is hope;
don't be a willing party to his death.
19 A hot-tempered man must pay the penalty,
for if you rescue him, you must do it again.
20 Listen to counsel and receive instruction,
that you may be wise in your latter end.
21 There are many plans in a man's heart,
but Yahweh's counsel will prevail.
22 That which makes a man to be desired is his kindness.
A poor man is better than a liar.
23 The fear of Yahweh leads to life, then contentment;
he rests and will not be touched by trouble.
24 The sluggard buries his hand in the dish;
he will not so much as bring it to his mouth again.
25 Flog a scoffer, and the simple will learn prudence;
rebuke one who has understanding, and he will gain knowledge.
26 He who robs his father and drives away his mother
is a son who causes shame and brings reproach.
27 If you stop listening to instruction, my son,
you will stray from the words of knowledge.
28 A corrupt witness mocks justice,
and the mouth of the wicked gulps down iniquity.
29 Penalties are prepared for scoffers,
and beatings for the backs of fools.

Day 19 – Whispers

Proverbs 19 — Slow Down, You're Rushing Grace

"Also it is not good to have zeal without knowledge, nor be hasty with one's feet and miss the way."

— Proverbs 19:2 (WEB)

Reflection:

Sometimes you're moving too fast to hear God's whisper.
    Haste ain't holy.
    Busyness don't equal breakthrough.
    Don't confuse passion with permission.
    Don't mistake movement for mission.
    Slow feet find wisdom.
    Hasty steps hit the wall.
    Let your soul breathe.
    Let your spirit check the GPS.
    Because it's better to be delayed in purpose
    Than on time to a mistake.
    Selah.

Sunrise: Stop Shrinking to Fit

She used to shrink so others felt big. Now she just shines.
He stopped apologizing for taking up space.
They walked tall, even when the room leaned small.
Your fullness is not a threat—it's a blessing.
Stop shrinking to fit. You were born to stand out.

<u>Sunset: You Deserve the Whole Room</u>

She stopped folding herself into corners.
He took up space in the room—and in his dreams.
They didn't apologize for the volume of their light.
You don't have to earn belonging. You already do.
You deserve the whole room. And the next one, too.

Proverbs 20

1 Wine is a mocker and beer is a brawler.
  Whoever is led astray by them is not wise.
  2 The terror of a king is like the roaring of a lion.
  He who provokes him to anger forfeits his own life.
  3 It is an honor for a man to keep aloof from strife,
  but every fool will be quarreling.
  4 The sluggard will not plow by reason of the winter;
  therefore he shall beg in harvest, and have nothing.
  5 Counsel in the heart of man is like deep water,
  but a man of understanding will draw it out.
  6 Many men claim to be men of unfailing love,
  but who can find a faithful man?
  7 A righteous man walks in integrity.
  Blessed are his children after him.
  8 A king who sits on the throne of judgment
  scatters away all evil with his eyes.
  9 Who can say, "I have made my heart pure.
  I am clean and without sin"?
  10 Differing weights and differing measures,
  both of them alike are an abomination to Yahweh.
  11 Even a child makes himself known by his doings,
  whether his work is pure, and whether it is right.
  12 The hearing ear, and the seeing eye,
  Yahweh has made even both of them.
  13 Don't love sleep, lest you come to poverty.
  Open your eyes, and you shall be satisfied with bread.

14 "It's no good, it's no good," says the buyer;
but when he is gone his way, then he boasts.
15 There is gold and abundance of rubies,
but the lips of knowledge are a rare jewel.
16 Take the garment of one who puts up collateral for a stranger;
and hold him in pledge for a wayward woman.
17 Fraudulent food is sweet to a man,
but afterwards his mouth is filled with gravel.
18 Plans are established by advice;
by wise guidance you wage war!
19 He who goes about as a tale-bearer reveals secrets;
therefore don't keep company with him who opens wide his lips.
20 Whoever curses his father or his mother,
his lamp shall be put out in blackness of darkness.
21 An inheritance quickly gained at the beginning
won't be blessed in the end.
22 Don't say, "I will pay back evil."
Wait for Yahweh, and he will save you.
23 Yahweh detests differing weights,
and dishonest scales are not pleasing.
24 A man's steps are from Yahweh;
how then can man understand his way?
25 It is a snare to a man to make a rash dedication,
then later to consider his vows.
26 A wise king winnows out the wicked,
and drives the threshing wheel over them.
27 The spirit of man is Yahweh's lamp,
searching all his innermost parts.
28 Love and faithfulness keep the king safe.
His throne is sustained by love.
29 The glory of young men is their strength.
The splendor of old men is their gray hair.
30 Wounding blows cleanse away evil,
and beatings purge the innermost parts.

Day 20 – Whispers

Proverbs 20 — Wait on It

"Don't say, 'I will pay back evil.' Wait for Yahweh, and he will save you."
— Proverbs 20:22 (WEB)

Reflection:

Revenge is heavy. Let God carry it.
    You don't have to match their mess.
    You don't have to avenge yourself to prove your worth.
    God sees. God knows.
    And trust? Trust is laying your sword down
    When every part of you wants to swing.
    Waiting isn't weakness.
    It's war strategy.
    And God's justice hits different—deep, clean, and right on time.
    So wait, beloved.
    You ain't forgotten. You're fortified.
    Selah.

Sunrise: Trust Yourself First

She double-checked her intuition—and it was right the first time.
He stopped outsourcing his gut feelings.
They realized the answers were already inside.
Trust isn't always about others. It starts with you.
Trust yourself first. You've got divine GPS built in.

Sunset: You Knew All Along

She remembered the first whisper—and wished she listened sooner.
He let himself be guided by peace, not pressure.
They made decisions that felt soft, but landed strong.
Your knowing is enough. You don't need proof.
You knew all along. Now it's safe to trust that voice.

Proverbs 21

1 The king's heart is in Yahweh's hand like the watercourses.
He turns it wherever he desires.
2 Every way of a man is right in his own eyes,
but Yahweh weighs the hearts.
3 To do righteousness and justice
is more acceptable to Yahweh than sacrifice.
4 A high look and a proud heart,
the lamp of the wicked, is sin.
5 The plans of the diligent surely lead to profit;
and everyone who is hasty surely rushes to poverty.
6 Getting treasures by a lying tongue
is a fleeting vapor for those who seek death.
7 The violence of the wicked will drive them away,
because they refuse to do what is right.
8 The way of the guilty is devious,
but the conduct of the innocent is upright.
9 It is better to dwell in the corner of the housetop
than to share a house with a contentious woman.
10 The soul of the wicked desires evil;
his neighbor finds no mercy in his eyes.
11 When the mocker is punished, the simple gains wisdom.
When the wise is instructed, he receives knowledge.
12 The Righteous One considers the house of the wicked,
and brings the wicked to ruin.
13 Whoever stops his ears at the cry of the poor,
he will also cry out, but shall not be heard.

14 A gift in secret pacifies anger,
and a bribe in the cloak, strong wrath.
15 It is joy to the righteous to do justice;
but it is a destruction to the workers of iniquity.
16 The man who wanders out of the way of understanding
shall rest in the assembly of the departed spirits.
17 He who loves pleasure will be a poor man.
He who loves wine and oil won't be rich.
18 The wicked is a ransom for the righteous,
the treacherous for the upright.
19 It is better to dwell in a desert land,
than with a contentious and fretful woman.
20 There is precious treasure and oil in the dwelling of the wise,
but a foolish man swallows it up.
21 He who follows after righteousness and kindness
finds life, righteousness, and honor.
22 A wise man scales the city of the mighty,
and brings down the strength of its confidence.
23 Whoever guards his mouth and his tongue
keeps his soul from troubles.
24 The proud and arrogant man—"Scoffer" is his name—
he works in the arrogance of pride.
25 The desire of the sluggard kills him,
for his hands refuse to labor.
26 There are those who covet greedily all day long;
but the righteous give and don't withhold.
27 The sacrifice of the wicked is an abomination—
how much more, when he brings it with a wicked mind!
28 A false witness will perish.
A man who listens speaks to eternity.
29 A wicked man hardens his face;
but as for the upright, he establishes his ways.
30 There is no wisdom nor understanding
nor counsel against Yahweh.
31 The horse is prepared for the day of battle;

but victory is with Yahweh.

Day 21 – Whispers

Proverbs 21 — God Sees the Motive, Not Just the Move

"Every way of a man is right in his own eyes, but Yahweh weighs the hearts."

— *Proverbs 21:2 (WEB)*

Reflection:

You might look righteous on the surface—tight speech, tidy plans, clean reputation.

But God don't check the resume. He checks the reasons.

You can fake the fruit, but not the root.

Because what He's weighing ain't just what you did—

It's why.

You don't have to be perfect.

Just honest.

Just surrendered.

Let your motives be mirrors, not masks.

Selah.

Shame Is Not Your Story

She stopped apologizing for surviving.

He let go of the labels they gave him.

They rewrote the narrative in love, not judgment.

Shame is loud—but it ain't wise.

Shame is not your story. Reclaim your pen.

<u>Sunrise: Shame Is Not Your Story</u>

She stopped apologizing for surviving.
    He let go of the labels they gave him.
    They rewrote the narrative in love, not judgment.
    Shame is loud—but it ain't wise.
        Shame is not your story. Reclaim your pen.

Sunset: Release What Wasn't Yours

She gave back the shame with a bow and a boundary.
    He laid down what was never his truth.
    They stepped out of guilt like an old coat that didn't fit.
    Healing is heavy—but so is holding what ain't yours.
    Release it all. Breathe lighter.

Proverbs 22

1 A good name is more desirable than great riches,
and loving favor is better than silver and gold.
2 The rich and the poor have this in common:
Yahweh is the maker of them all.
3 A prudent man sees danger and hides himself;
but the simple pass on, and suffer for it.
4 The result of humility and the fear of Yahweh
is wealth, honor, and life.
5 Thorns and snares are in the path of the wicked;
whoever guards his soul stays far from them.
6 Train up a child in the way he should go,
and when he is old he will not depart from it.
7 The rich rule over the poor.
The borrower is servant to the lender.
8 He who sows wickedness reaps trouble,
and the rod of his fury will be destroyed.
9 He who has a generous eye will be blessed,
for he shares his food with the poor.
10 Drive out the mocker, and strife will go out;
yes, quarrels and insults will stop.
11 He who loves purity of heart and speaks gracefully
is the king's friend.
12 Yahweh's eyes watch over knowledge,
but he frustrates the words of the unfaithful.
13 The sluggard says, "There is a lion outside!
I will be killed in the streets!"

14 The mouth of an adulteress is a deep pit.

He who is under Yahweh's wrath will fall into it.

15 Folly is bound up in the heart of a child;

the rod of discipline drives it far from him.

16 Whoever oppresses the poor for his own increase and whoever gives to the rich,

both come to poverty.

17 Turn your ear, and listen to the words of the wise.

Apply your heart to my teaching.

18 For it is a pleasant thing if you keep them within you,

if all of them are ready on your lips.

19 I teach you today, even you,

so that your trust may be in Yahweh.

20 Haven't I written to you thirty excellent things

of counsel and knowledge,

21 To teach you truth, reliable words,

to give sound answers to the ones who sent you?

22 Don't exploit the poor because he is poor;

and don't crush the needy in court;

23 for Yahweh will plead their case,

and plunder the life of those who plunder them.

24 Don't befriend a hot-tempered man.

Don't associate with one who harbors anger,

25 lest you learn his ways

and ensnare your soul.

26 Don't you be one of those who strike hands,

of those who are collateral for debts.

27 If you don't have means to pay,

why should he take away your bed from under you?

28 Don't move the ancient boundary stone

which your fathers have set up.

29 Do you see a man skilled in his work?

He will serve kings.

He won't serve obscure men.

Day 22 – Whispers

Proverbs 22 — A Good Name Ain't Cheap

"A good name is more desirable than great riches; loving favor is better than silver and gold."

— Proverbs 22:1 (WEB)

Reflection:

Money can buy you things.

But character gets you invited into rooms no coin can unlock.

Your name is a currency.

Spend it wisely.

Protect it fiercely.

Don't trade your reputation for applause.

Don't mortgage your integrity for a quick come-up.

Be the kind of person people speak well of even when you ain't in the room.

Let your name ring like honor, not noise.

Selah.

Sunrise: Slowness Is Sacred

She stretched before she scrolled. That was the first miracle.
He sipped his coffee like it was ceremony.
They watched the sunrise without recording it.
Fast ain't always wise. Loud ain't always right.
Slowness is sacred. Let it lead today.

Sunset: You're Not Missing Out

She skipped the chaos and found clarity.
He stayed home—and found home inside.
They missed the party—but met their peace.
You didn't miss out. You opted in to stillness.
You're not missing out. You're making space for what's real.

Proverbs 23

1 When you sit to eat with a ruler,
  consider diligently what is before you;
  2 put a knife to your throat
  if you are a man given to appetite.
  3 Don't be desirous of his dainties,
  since they are deceitful food.
  4 Don't weary yourself to be rich.
  In your wisdom, show restraint.
  5 Why do you set your eyes on that which is not?
  For it certainly sprouts wings like an eagle and flies in the sky.
  6 Don't eat the food of him who has a stingy eye,
  and don't crave his delicacies,
  7 for as he thinks about the cost, so he is.
  "Eat and drink!" he says to you,
  but his heart is not with you.
  8 You will vomit up the morsel which you have eaten
  and waste your pleasant words.
  9 Don't speak in the ears of a fool,
  for he will despise the wisdom of your words.
  10 Don't move the ancient boundary stone.
  Don't encroach on the fields of the fatherless,
  11 for their Defender is strong.
  He will plead their case against you.
  12 Apply your heart to instruction,
  and your ears to the words of knowledge.
  13 Don't withhold correction from a child.

If you punish him with the rod, he will not die.
14 Punish him with the rod,
and save his soul from Sheol.†[1]
15 My son, if your heart is wise,
then my heart will be glad, even mine.
16 Yes, my heart will rejoice
when your lips speak what is right.
17 Don't let your heart envy sinners,
but rather fear Yahweh all day long.
18 Indeed surely there is a future hope,
and your hope will not be cut off.
19 Listen, my son, and be wise,
and keep your heart on the right path!
20 Don't be among ones drinking too much wine,
or those who gorge themselves on meat;
21 for the drunkard and the glutton shall become poor;
and drowsiness clothes them in rags.
22 Listen to your father who gave you life,
and don't despise your mother when she is old.
23 Buy the truth, and don't sell it.
Get wisdom, discipline, and understanding.
24 The father of the righteous has great joy.
Whoever fathers a wise child delights in him.
25 Let your father and your mother be glad!
Let her who bore you rejoice!
26 My son, give me your heart;
and let your eyes keep in my ways.
27 For a prostitute is a deep pit;
and a wayward wife is a narrow well.
28 Yes, she lies in wait like a robber,
and increases the unfaithful among men.
29 Who has woe?
Who has sorrow?
Who has strife?

1.   https://ebible.org/eng-web/PRO23.htm#FN1

Who has complaints?
Who has needless bruises?
Who has bloodshot eyes?
30 Those who stay long at the wine;
those who go to seek out mixed wine.
31 Don't look at the wine when it is red,
when it sparkles in the cup,
when it goes down smoothly.
32 In the end, it bites like a snake,
and poisons like a viper.
33 Your eyes will see strange things,
and your mind will imagine confusing things.
34 Yes, you will be as he who lies down in the middle of the sea,
or as he who lies on top of the rigging:
35 "They hit me, and I was not hurt!
They beat me, and I don't feel it!
When will I wake up? I can do it again.
I will look for more."

Day 23 – Whispers

Proverbs 23 — Don't Get Drunk on Delusion

> *"Don't let your heart envy sinners, but rather fear Yahweh all day long."*
> *— Proverbs 23:17 (WEB)*

Reflection:

It might look like they winning.

Dripping in success, iced out in applause.
But don't envy the glitter, beloved.
Gold-plated don't mean God-ordained.
There's a quiet richness in righteousness.
There's a peace that envy can't touch.
Stay rooted in reverence.
Let your joy grow from within.
Because what's real don't need to flex.
And what's holy won't make you hustle your soul.
Selah.

Sunrise: Love Yourself Out Loud

She looked in the mirror and said, "Damn, I'm divine."
He gave himself grace before he gave anyone else his time.
They dressed like every room was their runway.
Self-love ain't selfish. It's sacred.
Love yourself out loud. You deserve to hear it, too.

Sunset: You've Always Been Enough

She remembered who she was—and it felt like coming home.
He laid down the lies and picked up his peace.
They no longer begged to belong.
You were born whole. You don't need fixing.
You've always been enough. Even before the glow-up.

Proverbs 24

1 Don't be envious of evil men,
  neither desire to be with them;
  2 for their hearts plot violence
  and their lips talk about mischief.
  3 Through wisdom a house is built;
  by understanding it is established;
  4 by knowledge the rooms are filled
  with all rare and beautiful treasure.
  5 A wise man has great power.
  A knowledgeable man increases strength,
  6 for by wise guidance you wage your war,
  and victory is in many advisors.
  7 Wisdom is too high for a fool.
  He doesn't open his mouth in the gate.
  8 One who plots to do evil
  will be called a schemer.
  9 The schemes of folly are sin.
  The mocker is detested by men.
  10 If you falter in the time of trouble,
  your strength is small.
  11 Rescue those who are being led away to death!
  Indeed, hold back those who are staggering to the slaughter!
  12 If you say, "Behold, we didn't know this,"
  doesn't he who weighs the hearts consider it?
  He who keeps your soul, doesn't he know it?
  Shall he not give to every man according to his work?

13 My son, eat honey, for it is good,
the droppings of the honeycomb, which are sweet to your taste;
14 so you shall know wisdom to be to your soul.
If you have found it, then there will be a reward:
Your hope will not be cut off.
15 Don't lay in wait, wicked man, against the habitation of the righteous.
Don't destroy his resting place;
16 for a righteous man falls seven times and rises up again,
but the wicked are overthrown by calamity.
17 Don't rejoice when your enemy falls.
Don't let your heart be glad when he is overthrown,
18 lest Yahweh see it, and it displease him,
and he turn away his wrath from him.
19 Don't fret yourself because of evildoers,
neither be envious of the wicked;
20 for there will be no reward to the evil man.
The lamp of the wicked will be snuffed out.
21 My son, fear Yahweh and the king.
Don't join those who are rebellious,
22 for their calamity will rise suddenly.
Who knows what destruction may come from them both?
23 These also are sayings of the wise:
To show partiality in judgment is not good.
24 He who says to the wicked, "You are righteous,"
peoples will curse him, and nations will abhor him—
25 but it will go well with those who convict the guilty,
and a rich blessing will come on them.
26 An honest answer
is like a kiss on the lips.
27 Prepare your work outside,
and get your fields ready.
Afterwards, build your house.
28 Don't be a witness against your neighbor without cause.
Don't deceive with your lips.
29 Don't say, "I will do to him as he has done to me;

I will repay the man according to his work."
30 I went by the field of the sluggard,
by the vineyard of the man void of understanding.
31 Behold, it was all grown over with thorns.
Its surface was covered with nettles,
and its stone wall was broken down.
32 Then I saw, and considered well.
I saw, and received instruction:
33 a little sleep, a little slumber,
a little folding of the hands to sleep,
34 so your poverty will come as a robber
and your want as an armed man.

Day 24 – Whispers

Proverbs 24 — Rise Anyway

"For a righteous man falls seven times and rises up again, but the wicked are overthrown by calamity."

— Proverbs 24:16 (WEB)

Reflection:

You gon' fall.

    Hard sometimes. Embarrassing sometimes.

    But the righteous ain't the ones who never trip—

    They're the ones who get back up. Again. And again.

    Failure ain't fatal when your faith's still intact.

    Your bounce-back got power.

    Your comeback is divine muscle memory.

    Fall seven.

    Rise eight.

    Selah.

Sunrise: Celebrate How Far You've Come

She looked back only to see how far she's grown.
He toasted to tiny wins and quiet survival.
They honored every scar like a badge of becoming.
Growth don't always shout—it sometimes sighs with relief.
Celebrate how far you've come. It's holy work.

<u>Sunset: Rest Is a Reward, Not a Rerun</u>

She didn't earn rest—she embraced it.
He closed the laptop like it was a sacred ritual.
They didn't try to "catch up"—they caught their breath.
Rest isn't laziness. It's legacy work.
Rest is a reward. Receive it.

Proverbs 25

^{1} Don't be envious of evil men,
    neither desire to be with them;

    ^{2} for their hearts plot violence
    and their lips talk about mischief.

    ^{3} Through wisdom a house is built;
    by understanding it is established;

    ^{4} by knowledge the rooms are filled
    with all rare and beautiful treasure.

    ^{5} A wise man has great power.
    A knowledgeable man increases strength,

    ^{6} for by wise guidance you wage your war,
    and victory is in many advisors.

    ^{7} Wisdom is too high for a fool.
    He doesn't open his mouth in the gate.

    ^{8} One who plots to do evil
    will be called a schemer.

    ^{9} The schemes of folly are sin.
    The mocker is detested by men.

    ^{10} If you falter in the time of trouble,
    your strength is small.

    ^{11} Rescue those who are being led away to death!
    Indeed, hold back those who are staggering to the slaughter!

^{12} If you say, "Behold, we didn't know this,"
doesn't he who weighs the hearts consider it?
He who keeps your soul, doesn't he know it?
Shall he not give to every man according to his work?

^{13} My son, eat honey, for it is good,
the droppings of the honeycomb, which are sweet to your taste;

^{14} so you shall know wisdom to be to your soul.
If you have found it, then there will be a reward:
Your hope will not be cut off.

^{15} Don't lay in wait, wicked man, against the habitation of the righteous.
Don't destroy his resting place;

^{16} for a righteous man falls seven times and rises up again,
but the wicked are overthrown by calamity.

^{17} Don't rejoice when your enemy falls.
Don't let your heart be glad when he is overthrown,

^{18} lest Yahweh see it, and it displease him,
and he turn away his wrath from him.

^{19} Don't fret yourself because of evildoers,
neither be envious of the wicked;

^{20} for there will be no reward to the evil man.
The lamp of the wicked will be snuffed out.

^{21} My son, fear Yahweh and the king.
Don't join those who are rebellious,

^{22} for their calamity will rise suddenly.
Who knows what destruction may come from them both?

^{23} These also are sayings of the wise:
To show partiality in judgment is not good.

^{24} He who says to the wicked, "You are righteous,"
peoples will curse him, and nations will abhor him—

^{25} but it will go well with those who convict the guilty,
and a rich blessing will come on them.

²⁶ An honest answer
is like a kiss on the lips.

²⁷ Prepare your work outside,
and get your fields ready.
Afterwards, build your house.

²⁸ Don't be a witness against your neighbor without cause.
Don't deceive with your lips.

²⁹ Don't say, "I will do to him as he has done to me;
I will repay the man according to his work."

³⁰ I went by the field of the sluggard,
by the vineyard of the man void of understanding.

³¹ Behold, it was all grown over with thorns.
Its surface was covered with nettles,
and its stone wall was broken down.

³² Then I saw, and considered well.
I saw, and received instruction:

³³ a little sleep, a little slumber,
a little folding of the hands to sleep,

³⁴ so your poverty will come as a robber
and your want as an armed man.

Day 25 – Whispers

Proverbs 25 — Apples of Gold, Words on Time

"A word fitly spoken is like apples of gold in settings of silver."
— Proverbs 25:11 (WEB)

Reflection:

Some words hit like healing.
 Like a soft balm on a bruised ego.
 Like sunlight after the storm's tantrum.
 The right word at the right time?
 That's holy.
 Don't just aim to be loud—aim to be *timely*.
 Don't rush to speak—wait to bless.
 Because when you open your mouth with grace,
 You feed folks in ways food never could.
 Let your language glisten with gold.
 Let your voice be velvet and wisdom wrapped in one.
 Selah.

Sunrise: You Are the Answer to Somebody's Prayer

She showed up not knowing who was watching—just that it mattered.

He smiled at a stranger. And changed a whole day.

They made space where there was none.

You might not feel like a blessing—but you are.

You are the answer to somebody's prayer. Walk like it.

Sunset: You're a Living Legacy

She lit a candle and it lit a generation.

He broke cycles with a single boundary.

They carried traditions in their laughter.

Legacy ain't always loud. Sometimes it hums soft and steady.

You're a living legacy.

Even in your rest.

Proverbs 26

1 Like snow in summer, and as rain in harvest,
so honor is not fitting for a fool.
2 Like a fluttering sparrow,
like a darting swallow,
so the undeserved curse doesn't come to rest.
3 A whip is for the horse,
a bridle for the donkey,
and a rod for the back of fools!
4 Don't answer a fool according to his folly,
lest you also be like him.
5 Answer a fool according to his folly,
lest he be wise in his own eyes.
6 One who sends a message by the hand of a fool
is cutting off feet and drinking violence.
7 Like the legs of the lame that hang loose,
so is a parable in the mouth of fools.
8 As one who binds a stone in a sling,
so is he who gives honor to a fool.
9 Like a thorn bush that goes into the hand of a drunkard,
so is a parable in the mouth of fools.
10 As an archer who wounds all,
so is he who hires a fool
or he who hires those who pass by.
11 As a dog that returns to his vomit,
so is a fool who repeats his folly.
12 Do you see a man wise in his own eyes?

There is more hope for a fool than for him.
13 The sluggard says, "There is a lion in the road!
A fierce lion roams the streets!"
14 As the door turns on its hinges,
so does the sluggard on his bed.
15 The sluggard buries his hand in the dish.
He is too lazy to bring it back to his mouth.
16 The sluggard is wiser in his own eyes
than seven men who answer with discretion.
17 Like one who grabs a dog's ears
is one who passes by and meddles in a quarrel not his own.
18 Like a madman who shoots torches, arrows, and death,
19 is the man who deceives his neighbor and says, "Am I not joking?"
20 For lack of wood a fire goes out.
Without gossip, a quarrel dies down.
21 As coals are to hot embers,
and wood to fire,
so is a contentious man to kindling strife.
22 The words of a whisperer are as dainty morsels,
they go down into the innermost parts.
23 Like silver dross on an earthen vessel
are the lips of a fervent one with an evil heart.
24 A malicious man disguises himself with his lips,
but he harbors evil in his heart.
25 When his speech is charming, don't believe him,
for there are seven abominations in his heart.
26 His malice may be concealed by deception,
but his wickedness will be exposed in the assembly.
27 Whoever digs a pit shall fall into it.
Whoever rolls a stone, it will come back on him.
28 A lying tongue hates those it hurts;
and a flattering mouth works ruin.

Day 26 – Whispers

Proverbs 26 — Don't Feed the Fool

"Don't answer a fool according to his folly, lest you also be like him."
— Proverbs 26:4 (WEB)

Reflection:

Some arguments ain't worth your oxygen.

Not every fool deserves a forum.

Silence is not surrender—it's strategy.

Because when you try to school someone who loves their own echo,

You end up playing in their circus.

Let them juggle their own nonsense.

You got peace to protect.

You got wisdom that don't need to yell.

Choose when to speak.

And more importantly—choose when not to.

Selah.

Sunrise: Reclaim Your Joy

She stopped waiting for permission to be happy.
    He laughed louder than the lie that said he couldn't.
    They danced without the music—because joy lives inside.
    Joy is not something to earn. It's something to return to.
    Reclaim your joy. It missed you.

<u>Sunset: Joy Is Still Yours</u>

She found joy tucked inside a quiet breath.
    He smiled at the sky, no reason needed.
    They let joy share the bed with grief—and it still fit.
    Joy doesn't leave. We just forget to notice it.
    Joy is still yours. Even now.

Proverbs 27

1 Don't boast about tomorrow;
  for you don't know what a day may bring.
  2 Let another man praise you,
  and not your own mouth;
  a stranger, and not your own lips.
  3 A stone is heavy,
  and sand is a burden;
  but a fool's provocation is heavier than both.
  4 Wrath is cruel,
  and anger is overwhelming;
  but who is able to stand before jealousy?
  5 Better is open rebuke
  than hidden love.
  6 The wounds of a friend are faithful,
  although the kisses of an enemy are profuse.
  7 A full soul loathes a honeycomb;
  but to a hungry soul, every bitter thing is sweet.
  8 As a bird that wanders from her nest,
  so is a man who wanders from his home.
  9 Perfume and incense bring joy to the heart;
  so does earnest counsel from a man's friend.
  10 Don't forsake your friend and your father's friend.
  Don't go to your brother's house in the day of your disaster.
  A neighbor who is near is better than a distant brother.
  11 Be wise, my son,
  and bring joy to my heart,

then I can answer my tormentor.

12 A prudent man sees danger and takes refuge;
but the simple pass on, and suffer for it.

13 Take his garment when he puts up collateral for a stranger.
Hold it for a wayward woman!

14 He who blesses his neighbor with a loud voice early in the morning,
it will be taken as a curse by him.

15 A continual dropping on a rainy day
and a contentious wife are alike:

16 restraining her is like restraining the wind,
or like grasping oil in his right hand.

17 Iron sharpens iron;
so a man sharpens his friend's countenance.

18 Whoever tends the fig tree shall eat its fruit.
He who looks after his master shall be honored.

19 Like water reflects a face,
so a man's heart reflects the man.

20 Sheol†[1] and Abaddon are never satisfied;
and a man's eyes are never satisfied.

21 The crucible is for silver,
and the furnace for gold;
but man is refined by his praise.

22 Though you grind a fool in a mortar with a pestle along with grain,
yet his foolishness will not be removed from him.

23 Know well the state of your flocks,
and pay attention to your herds,

24 for riches are not forever,
nor does the crown endure to all generations.

25 The hay is removed, and the new growth appears,
the grasses of the hills are gathered in.

26 The lambs are for your clothing,
and the goats are the price of a field.

27 There will be plenty of goats' milk for your food,
for your family's food,

---

1.   https://ebible.org/eng-web/PRO27.htm#FN1

and for the nourishment of your servant girls.

Day 27 – Whispers

Proverbs 27 — Let the Work Speak

> *"Let another man praise you, and not your own mouth; a stranger, and not your own lips."*

> *— Proverbs 27:2 (WEB)*

Reflection:

You don't have to announce yourself.

Just show up. Shine. Stay consistent.

Let your fruit do the talking.

Let your work introduce you in rooms your resume can't.

You're not invisible because you're quiet.

You're powerful because you're grounded.

Let God do the PR.

You just be excellent.

Selah.

Sunrise: Divine Timing Is Real

She bloomed later—and brighter.
>He watched everyone else "win," and still waited in peace.
>They trusted the delay was divine design.
>What's for you won't miss you. It'll find you ready.
>Divine timing is real. Walk, don't chase.

<u>Sunset: Wait With Grace</u>

She stopped begging and started preparing.
>He lit a candle and waited for peace to fill the room.
>They paused the panic. And found calm underneath.
>Grace is the glow that holds you while you wait.
>Wait with grace. It's coming.

Proverbs 28

1 The wicked flee when no one pursues;
    but the righteous are as bold as a lion.
2 In rebellion, a land has many rulers,
    but order is maintained by a man of understanding and knowledge.
3 A needy man who oppresses the poor
    is like a driving rain which leaves no crops.
4 Those who forsake the law praise the wicked;
    but those who keep the law contend with them.
5 Evil men don't understand justice;
    but those who seek Yahweh understand it fully.
6 Better is the poor who walks in his integrity
    than he who is perverse in his ways, and he is rich.
7 Whoever keeps the law is a wise son;
    but he who is a companion of gluttons shames his father.
8 He who increases his wealth by excessive interest
    gathers it for one who has pity on the poor.
9 He who turns away his ear from hearing the law,
    even his prayer is an abomination.
10 Whoever causes the upright to go astray in an evil way,
    he will fall into his own trap;
    but the blameless will inherit good.
11 The rich man is wise in his own eyes;
    but the poor who has understanding sees through him.
12 When the righteous triumph, there is great glory;
    but when the wicked rise, men hide themselves.
13 He who conceals his sins doesn't prosper,

but whoever confesses and renounces them finds mercy.

14 Blessed is the man who always fears;

but one who hardens his heart falls into trouble.

15 As a roaring lion or a charging bear,

so is a wicked ruler over helpless people.

16 A tyrannical ruler lacks judgment.

One who hates ill-gotten gain will have long days.

17 A man who is tormented by blood guilt will be a fugitive until death.

No one will support him.

18 Whoever walks blamelessly is kept safe;

but one with perverse ways will fall suddenly.

19 One who works his land will have an abundance of food;

but one who chases fantasies will have his fill of poverty.

20 A faithful man is rich with blessings;

but one who is eager to be rich will not go unpunished.

21 To show partiality is not good,

yet a man will do wrong for a piece of bread.

22 A stingy man hurries after riches,

and doesn't know that poverty waits for him.

23 One who rebukes a man will afterward find more favor

than one who flatters with the tongue.

24 Whoever robs his father or his mother and says, "It's not wrong,"

is a partner with a destroyer.

25 One who is greedy stirs up strife;

but one who trusts in Yahweh will prosper.

26 One who trusts in himself is a fool;

but one who walks in wisdom is kept safe.

27 One who gives to the poor has no lack;

but one who closes his eyes will have many curses.

28 When the wicked rise, men hide themselves;

but when they perish, the righteous thrive.

Day 28 – Whispers

Proverbs 28 — Don't Be Scared of Goodness

"The wicked flee when no one pursues; but the righteous are as bold as a lion."

— Proverbs 28:1 (WEB)

Reflection:

When your heart is clean, you can walk boldly.
> You ain't gotta look over your shoulder.
> Ain't no guilt to dodge. No shadows chasing you.
> Wickedness makes people jumpy.
> But righteousness? It gives you a backbone.
> Step into the room like it's already yours.
> Speak like truth is your bodyguard.
> Live bold. Live clear. Live holy.
> You got no reason to run.
> Selah.

Sunrise: Own Your Power

She stopped shrinking and started shining.
He spoke his truth—and the air shifted.
They stood tall in rooms not built for them.
Power doesn't always roar. Sometimes it just is.
Own your power. It was never lost—just waiting.

<u>Sunset: You Were Powerful All Along</u>

She looked back and saw her strength in every step.
He stopped downplaying his greatness.
They let go of the fear of being "too much."
Power isn't something you chase. It's something you remember.
You were powerful all along. Now rest like you believe it.

Proverbs 29

1 He who is often rebuked and stiffens his neck
  will be destroyed suddenly, with no remedy.
  2 When the righteous thrive, the people rejoice;
  but when the wicked rule, the people groan.
  3 Whoever loves wisdom brings joy to his father;
  but a companion of prostitutes squanders his wealth.
  4 The king by justice makes the land stable,
  but he who takes bribes tears it down.
  5 A man who flatters his neighbor
  spreads a net for his feet.
  6 An evil man is snared by his sin,
  but the righteous can sing and be glad.
  7 The righteous care about justice for the poor.
  The wicked aren't concerned about knowledge.
  8 Mockers stir up a city,
  but wise men turn away anger.
  9 If a wise man goes to court with a foolish man,
  the fool rages or scoffs, and there is no peace.
  10 The bloodthirsty hate a man of integrity;
  and they seek the life of the upright.
  11 A fool vents all of his anger,
  but a wise man brings himself under control.
  12 If a ruler listens to lies,
  all of his officials are wicked.
  13 The poor man and the oppressor have this in common:
  Yahweh gives sight to the eyes of both.

14 The king who fairly judges the poor,
his throne shall be established forever.
15 The rod of correction gives wisdom,
but a child left to himself causes shame to his mother.
16 When the wicked increase, sin increases;
but the righteous will see their downfall.
17 Correct your son, and he will give you peace;
yes, he will bring delight to your soul.
18 Where there is no revelation, the people cast off restraint;
but one who keeps the law is blessed.
19 A servant can't be corrected by words.
Though he understands, yet he will not respond.
20 Do you see a man who is hasty in his words?
There is more hope for a fool than for him.
21 He who pampers his servant from youth
will have him become a son in the end.
22 An angry man stirs up strife,
and a wrathful man abounds in sin.
23 A man's pride brings him low,
but one of lowly spirit gains honor.
24 Whoever is an accomplice of a thief is an enemy of his own soul.
He takes an oath, but dares not testify.
25 The fear of man proves to be a snare,
but whoever puts his trust in Yahweh is kept safe.
26 Many seek the ruler's favor,
but a man's justice comes from Yahweh.
27 A dishonest man detests the righteous,
and the upright in their ways detest the wicked.

Day 29 – Whispers

Proverbs 29 — Don't Fear the People

"The fear of man proves to be a snare, but whoever puts his trust in Yahweh is kept safe."

— Proverbs 29:25 (WEB)

Reflection:

People-pleasing is a trap.
> A velvet rope that tightens until you can't breathe.
> Don't live your life auditioning for applause.
> Don't let other folks' opinions be your GPS.
> God's approval is the only one that frees you.
> Trust that.
> Move with that.
> Because being safe in God
> Beats being liked by man.
> Selah.

Sunrise: Hope Ain't Never Left You

She opened her curtains and found hope sitting in the sun.
   He whispered, "Maybe," and that was enough to keep going.
   They let hope ride shotgun—even when fear was driving.
   Hope ain't loud—but she stays.
   Hope ain't never left you. You just forgot her name.

<u>Sunset: Let the Light Tuck You In</u>

She didn't fake the smile. She rested her face and still felt joy.
   He didn't have answers—just breath. And that was enough.
   They stopped holding it all together—and nothing fell apart.
   Let love hold you like the night holds the moon.
   Let the light tuck you in. You've done enough. Be held.

Proverbs 30

1 The words of Agur the son of Jakeh, the revelation:
   the man says to Ithiel,
   to Ithiel and Ucal:
   2 "Surely I am the most ignorant man,
   and don't have a man's understanding.
   3 I have not learned wisdom,
   neither do I have the knowledge of the Holy One.
   4 Who has ascended up into heaven, and descended?
   Who has gathered the wind in his fists?
   Who has bound the waters in his garment?
   Who has established all the ends of the earth?
   What is his name, and what is his son's name, if you know?
   5 "Every word of God is flawless.
   He is a shield to those who take refuge in him.
   6 Don't you add to his words,
   lest he reprove you, and you be found a liar.
   7 "Two things I have asked of you.
   Don't deny me before I die.
   8 Remove far from me falsehood and lies.
   Give me neither poverty nor riches.
   Feed me with the food that is needful for me,
   9 lest I be full, deny you, and say, 'Who is Yahweh?'
   or lest I be poor, and steal,
   and so dishonor the name of my God.
   10 "Don't slander a servant to his master,
   lest he curse you, and you be held guilty.

11 There is a generation that curses their father,

and doesn't bless their mother.

12 There is a generation that is pure in their own eyes, yet are not washed from their filthiness.

13 There is a generation, oh how lofty are their eyes!

Their eyelids are lifted up.

14 There is a generation whose teeth are like swords,

and their jaws like knives,

to devour the poor from the earth, and the needy from among men.

15 "The leech has two daughters:

'Give, give.'

"There are three things that are never satisfied;

four that don't say, 'Enough!':

16 Sheol,†[1]

the barren womb,

the earth that is not satisfied with water,

and the fire that doesn't say, 'Enough!'

17 "The eye that mocks at his father,

and scorns obedience to his mother,

the ravens of the valley shall pick it out,

the young eagles shall eat it.

18 "There are three things which are too amazing for me, four which I don't understand:

19 The way of an eagle in the air,

the way of a serpent on a rock,

the way of a ship in the middle of the sea,

and the way of a man with a maiden.

20 "So is the way of an adulterous woman:

She eats and wipes her mouth,

and says, 'I have done nothing wrong.'

21 "For three things the earth trembles,

and under four, it can't bear up:

22 For a servant when he is king,

a fool when he is filled with food,

---

23 for an unloved woman when she is married,

and a servant who is heir to her mistress.

24 "There are four things which are little on the earth,

but they are exceedingly wise:

25 The ants are not a strong people,

yet they provide their food in the summer.

26 The hyraxes are but a feeble folk,

yet make they their houses in the rocks.

27 The locusts have no king,

yet they advance in ranks.

28 You can catch a lizard with your hands,

yet it is in kings' palaces.

29 "There are three things which are stately in their march, four which are stately in going:

30 The lion, which is mightiest among animals,

and doesn't turn away for any;

31 the greyhound; the male goat; and the king against whom there is no rising up.

32 "If you have done foolishly in lifting up yourself,

or if you have thought evil,

put your hand over your mouth.

33 For as the churning of milk produces butter,

and the wringing of the nose produces blood,

so the forcing of wrath produces strife."

Day 30 – Whispers

Proverbs 30 — The Wisdom of "I Don't Know"

"Surely I am the most ignorant man, and don't have a man's understanding. I have not learned wisdom, neither do I have the knowledge of the Holy One."

— Proverbs 30:2–3 (WEB)

Reflection:

The wisest thing you can say sometimes?

"I don't know."

This world got folks faking brilliance

Because they're scared to be seen as beginners.

But real wisdom bows low.

It asks questions. It honors mystery.

It knows that God ain't impressed by your overthinking—He's moved by your surrender.

Stay teachable.

Stay soft.

Stay humble enough to grow.

Selah.

Sunrise: Begin Again, On Purpose

She woke up softer, but stronger.

He packed light—left shame, fear, and guilt behind.

They didn't need a plan. Just a promise to try again.

Every sunrise is a second chance.

Begin again. But this time, begin as your whole self.

Sunset: You Are the Whisper Now

She became the calm she used to pray for.

He lit the torch for someone else to find their way.

They left a trail of peace wherever they walked.

You are someone's answered prayer. Someone's quiet strength.

You are the whisper now. Pass it on.

Proverbs 31

1 The words of King Lemuel—the revelation which his mother taught him:

2 "Oh, my son! Oh, son of my womb!

Oh, son of my vows!

3 Don't give your strength to women,

nor your ways to that which destroys kings.

4 It is not for kings, Lemuel,

it is not for kings to drink wine,

nor for princes to say, 'Where is strong drink?'

5 lest they drink, and forget the law,

and pervert the justice due to anyone who is afflicted.

6 Give strong drink to him who is ready to perish,

and wine to the bitter in soul.

7 Let him drink, and forget his poverty,

and remember his misery no more.

8 Open your mouth for the mute,

in the cause of all who are left desolate.

9 Open your mouth, judge righteously,

and serve justice to the poor and needy."

10 †[1]Who can find a worthy woman?

For her value is far above rubies.

11 The heart of her husband trusts in her.

He shall have no lack of gain.

12 She does him good, and not harm,

all the days of her life.

13 She seeks wool and flax,

---

1.   https://ebible.org/eng-web/PRO31.htm#FN1

and works eagerly with her hands.
14 She is like the merchant ships.
She brings her bread from afar.
15 She rises also while it is yet night,
gives food to her household,
and portions for her servant girls.
16 She considers a field, and buys it.
With the fruit of her hands, she plants a vineyard.
17 She arms her waist with strength,
and makes her arms strong.
18 She perceives that her merchandise is profitable.
Her lamp doesn't go out by night.
19 She lays her hands to the distaff,
and her hands hold the spindle.
20 She opens her arms to the poor;
yes, she extends her hands to the needy.
21 She is not afraid of the snow for her household,
for all her household are clothed with scarlet.
22 She makes for herself carpets of tapestry.
Her clothing is fine linen and purple.
23 Her husband is respected in the gates,
when he sits among the elders of the land.
24 She makes linen garments and sells them,
and delivers sashes to the merchant.
25 Strength and dignity are her clothing.
She laughs at the time to come.
26 She opens her mouth with wisdom.
Kind instruction is on her tongue.
27 She looks well to the ways of her household,
and doesn't eat the bread of idleness.
28 Her children rise up and call her blessed.
Her husband also praises her:
29 "Many women do noble things,
but you excel them all."
30 Charm is deceitful, and beauty is vain;

but a woman who fears Yahweh, she shall be praised.
31 Give her of the fruit of her hands!
Let her works praise her in the gates!

Day 31 – Whispers

Proverbs 31 — Crown Her

> *"Strength and dignity are her clothing. She laughs at the time to come... Her children rise up and call her blessed. Her husband also praises her... A woman who fears Yahweh, she shall be praised."*

> *— Proverbs 31:25, 28, 30 (WEB)*

Reflection:

She's not perfect—but she's powerful.
    Not flawless—but full of grace.
    She rises before the sun.
    She feeds, builds, speaks life.
    She handles business and still makes time to dance.
    Don't just read about her—*be* her.
    And when you see her out here grinding, glowing, giving her all?
    Crown her.
    Because she carries wisdom in her womb
    And legacy on her lips.
    Selah.

Sunrise: You Are the Blueprint

She rises while it's still dark—

because stars don't wait for sunrise.

He calls her blessed—

not because she serves, but because she leads.

They stand on her shoulders and still can't see her crown.

She speaks with wisdom, moves with grace, and laughs without fear of the future.

You are the blueprint, the builder, and the blessing. Walk like it.

Sunset: The Crown Fits

She did the work no one clapped for—and still shined.

He saw her light and didn't try to dim it—just reflected it back.

They whispered her name in rooms she hadn't even entered yet.

Charm fades. Beauty shifts. But character? That's eternal.

The crown fits. Rest, Queen. You've worn it well today.

Conclusion

31 days. 62 whispers. A whole healing journey.

From daybreak to dreamtime, you've created something *divine*—a daily practice, a sonic sanctuary, a mirror for those who forgot how powerful they are.

The Whisper Continues

If you've made it to this page, then let me say what maybe nobody has said to you lately:

I'm proud of you.

You showed up—for 30 days and 30 nights.

You made space for quiet in a noisy world.

You slowed down when everything told you to speed up.

You listened—to your breath, your truth, your God, your gut.

That's no small thing. That's everything.

This book may end here, but the whisper continues—in your choices, your rest, your joy, your boundaries, your prayers, your laughter. You are no longer just the one being whispered to.

You are the whisper.

Let your presence remind someone else they can exhale.

Let your softness interrupt the cycle.

Let your life be a loud yes to peace, purpose, and power.

And when you forget (because we all do)... come back.

Open a page.

Breathe in the truth again.

Because Whispers of Wisdom isn't just a book.

It's a returning.

A remembering.

A re-grounding.
So rise slow.
Rest soft.
And keep whispering—until the whole world listens.
With love,
Joseline Jean-Louis Hardrick
The Whisper. The Witness. The Word.

About the Author

Joseline Jean-Louis Hardrick is a lawyer, professor, storyteller, and seeker of balance in all things. Blending the discipline of law with the flow of poetry, she reimagines ancient wisdom for modern lives. Her work bridges cultures, generations, and worlds—inviting readers to find stillness in the swirl, strength in the soft, and joy in the journey.

Read more at www.joselinehardrick.com.